PRAISE FOR *THE EVERYDAY LEADER*

"As a professional coach that has been fortunate to have worked with some very successful teams at the highest levels, I have had the word leadership re-defined for me on numerous occasions. *The Everyday Leader* is an excellent read that hits the mark on so many levels; it paints a clear picture on the importrance of leadership in the 21st century, it provides real-world examples of ordinary people performing extraordinary tasks, and it is a commonsense example of how doing it right on a daily basis sets you up for success. I am in the leadership business and, at the end of the day, I believe people want to be led. *The Everyday Leader* is an authentic look at how living your life in accordance with a strong value system and having the courage to act can help you identify situations (however big or small) that provide leadership opportunities."

JAY WOODCROFT, *Professional Hockey Coach, Stanley Cup Winner '08, World Champion '15*

"If you're a leader looking to implement dynamic changes, this stimulating read will put you on the right track."

ANGUS THIRLWELL, *CEO and Co-founder, Hotel Chocolat*

"An honest and powerful examination of the responsibilities of those who aspire to lead others."

RANULPH FIENNES, *explorer and writer*

"An innovative, enjoyable, absorbing and original book that explores what leadership means and how it impacts others around you, both in the work and family arenas."

RICHARD KNIGHT OBE, *Chief Operating Officer, Newcastle International Airport*

"Highlights those moments in every day when we all have the power to affect outcomes more positively. Brilliantly accessible advice."

MARSHALL GOLDSMITH, *New York Times #1 bestselling author of* Triggers, Mojo, *and* What Got You Here Won't Get You There

"Brings leadership to life and certainly hits the mark with an array of positive guidance pointers to enhance your 'Everyday' leadership."

NICK DEAN, *Chief Constable of Cambridgeshire Constabulary*

"A modern-day Dale Carnegie, this book will help you lead fearlessly in life and in work. Unmissable!"

VICKI PSARIAS, *bestselling author of* Mumboss *and founder of Honestmum.com*

"John, Rafael and Kevin have done a brilliant job in bringing together real life leadership stories with short academic explanations."

MALCOLM DIAMOND MBE, *Chairman, Trifast Plc, DiscoverIE Plc and Flowtech Fluidpower Plc*

"This book is full of practical examples that help me lead my business everyday."

SAM DREYER, *CEO, Antidote Events*

"This book strikes the balance between rigour and relevance perfectly. It is packed with practical wisdom: great examples that are based on theories that don't get in the way of the practical insights."

DR IRENE GARNELO-GOMEZ, *Lecturer in Reputation and Sustainability at the University of Reading*

THE EVERYDAY LEADER

THE EVERYDAY LEADER

How to Motivate, Empower and Influence Those Around You

JOHN CROSS, RAFAEL GOMEZ
AND KEVIN MONEY

BLOOMSBURY BUSINESS
LONDON • NEW YORK • OXFORD • NEW DELHI • SYDNEY

BLOOMSBURY BUSINESS
Bloomsbury Publishing Plc
50 Bedford Square, London, WC1B 3DP, UK
1385 Broadway, New York, NY 10018, USA

BLOOMSBURY, BLOOMSBURY BUSINESS and the Diana logo are trademarks of Bloomsbury Publishing Plc

First published in Great Britain 2019

Cover design by Alice Marwick

A catalogue record for this book is available from the British Library.

A catalog record for this book is available from the Library of Congress.

ISBN: HB: 978-1-4729-6574-5
ePDF: 978-1-4729-6572-1
eBook: 978-1-4729-6575-2

Typeset by RefineCatch Limited, Bungay, Suffolk
Printed and bound in Great Britain

To find out more about our authors and books visit www.bloomsbury.com and sign up for our newsletters.

CONTENTS

ABOUT THE AUTHORS

John Cross, Rafael Gomez and Kevin Money co-wrote *'The Little Black Book for Managers'* published by John Wiley & Sons in 2013.

John Cross

Now semi-retired John has spent nearly twenty years as a leadership and management consultant to large organisations in both the public and private sectors. With his co-authors he has designed learning and development programmes for his clients' middle managers and senior executives and delivered them around the world to audiences of mixed ethnicity in the Americas, the Far East, Middle East and Europe. Customers included HP and BT etc. John is an executive coach, and a guest speaker at Henley Business School, the London School of Economics, and on the Cunard cruise ship line. He lives with his wife Julia in Cambridge, England. They have three children and ten grandchildren. Both support Arsenal football club. John is a qualified fixed-wing and helicopter pilot, and during the writing this book, passed his driving test for articulated large goods vehicles.

Professor Rafael Gomez MA, MIR, PhD

Rafael has a BA and Masters in Economics and a Masters and PhD in Industrial Relations. Since receiving his PhD he has taught and/or conducted research at various international institutions such as the London School of Economics, the Central Bank of Spain, and

Glendon College (York University). Since 2009 he has been Professor of Employment Relations at the University of Toronto and is currently the Director of the Centre for Industrial Relations and Human Resources. He is the author of several books and over 70 articles and chapters in edited volumes. Rafael also co-founded ThinkTankToronto in 2004 – a social enterprise that brings together a wealth of academic, consulting, corporate communication and public policy experience and expertise – and is the current Director. He is fluent in French and Spanish. Rafael lives with his wife Trish and their two children in Toronto, Canada..

Professor Kevin Money BSc, MSc, PhD, C.Psychol

Kevin Money is the Director of the John Madejski Centre for Reputation and Professor of Reputation and Responsible Leadership at Henley Business School. Kevin is a Chartered Psychologist and former Editor of the Journal of General Management and Manager Update. He is also a director of several organisations, including the Positive Psychology Forum. He is the author of numerous publications in outlets such as the Journal of Business Research, Group and Organisation Management, the Journal of Business Ethics, the British Journal of Management and the Harvard Business Manager. He is a frequent speaker at international conferences and a keen supervisor for doctoral research. Kevin is also recognised as a leading international consultant and has led projects with both public and private sector organisations including Shell, Unilever and Zurich Insurance as well as working with governments, the civil service and not-for-profit organisations. In 2014 he was appointed as a member of the Evaluation Council of the UK Cabinet and Prime Ministers' Office – and was a key contributor to the Evaluation Framework 2.0 that was published in 2018.

Kevin lives in Henley-on-Thames with Carola and their two children.

Introduction

You're happily driving along, when you notice in the rear view mirror a car coming up behind you. It gets so close that you feel the pressure to increase your speed. Or you're standing in line at the supermarket and the person behind you gradually invades your personal space until you feel the pressure to move forward. In both scenarios, people are trying deliberately to lead your physical reaction by applying emotional pressure; bullying or harassment, you could say. I pull up behind a van blocking the road ahead and wait for the oncoming car to pass. I wait for a signal of thanks from the passing driver, a raised hand or a flash of lights, but don't receive any acknowledgment of my consideration. That driver too has led my emotional reaction but maybe not as deliberately or consciously as the two previous examples.

I wonder how you would feel if you discovered that it was the same tailgater or queue presser that subsequently visited your house to help you with your investments and pension plans. I imagine you'd consider going somewhere else for advice. Even if they were the best-rated financial adviser in the industry, your previous experience means that their reputation, for you, is a little tarnished.

Everyone has a reputation which they have earned over time through a combination of conscious conduct and more frequently by unconscious omission. People can be generally classified as mostly 'givers' or mostly 'takers' and entire industries have a reputation; some poor, such as politics, car sales and utility companies; others good, such as teaching and nursing.

You have a reputation and it acts as the foundation and the basis for your potential ability to lead other people. Effective and successful leadership motivates and inspires. With a good reputation, you have earned the potential to lead an individual or to lead a nation. Others will travel with you towards your ambitious goal willingly and enthusiastically if the goal is deemed worthwhile. Without the reputation or the worthwhile goal, incentives, bonuses, fear, coercion, even force, will be required to get people to do what you want.

Realistically, despots, tyrants and the self-obsessed are unlikely to buy this book, but many everyday leaders find it difficult to fashion a long-term vision or even a short-term goal that gets the whole-hearted support and commitment from their family, their work team or their organization. For the vast majority of people that is the key challenge. And that's why this book has been written.

When we wrote *The Little Black Book for Managers*, published in 2013, we always had the intention of writing a book on leadership. But when speaking with different publishers subsequently, they informed us that there was a more limited audience for books on leadership, as the majority of people don't think of themselves as leaders. We thought that was wrong. Everybody has a reputation and with it, the potential to lead.

Yes, it's true that many ordinary people – parents, factory and office workers, those employed by government departments, charities and the like – think of leadership as something for which someone else is responsible, the boss at work, or their government. Those in the business world often look to the chief executive and the board for leadership. But this is not how the world actually works. This book explains that everyone, whether they recognize it or not, is a leader: a leader of emotions, of behaviours, of values, of beliefs even. So we set out to put together a series of recommendations for people who we have called 'everyday leaders'. In short, this will be a book for everyone in a leadership role, whether they presently recognize it or not.

In each chapter we refer to everyday leadership in the family unit; in social settings; in teams at work; and in organizations large and small, both commercial and not-for-profit. And we haven't forgotten the leaders of the free world and their governments either. So this book will focus on how every individual and every organization can steer those in their communities, be they individuals, families or giant corporations, towards a higher level of conscious behaviour and therefore better outcomes.

Our research has taken us into the boardrooms of public and private organizations to speak with those holding traditional leadership positions; into local coffee shops to speak with those who are effecting change within their local community; and into single family units to understand the relationship dynamics at work. We bring you the lessons that have been learned by these groups, more often than not, through repeated failures and disappointments, so that you have a better basis for your conscious decision making.

The Everyday Leader has been written during a period of political adjustment where a movement has emerged of electorates rejecting the liberal/parental leadership styles of Western democracies and instead showing support for leaders tuning into more fundamental emotional feelings. This book taps into this adjustment as it focuses more on the emotional connection between leaders and followers rather than just the intellectual one. Having said this, our true hope is that by promoting better leadership skills in as many people as possible – bottom up as well as top down – others will learn from your example. Right now, people who feel powerless are too readily attracted to simple leadership solutions rather than better, long-term ones that may, on the face of it, appear more complicated. We will help them navigate this leadership maze and avoid the blind alleys of reactionism and fear.

We believe that there is an urgent need for better leadership at all levels in the twenty-first century; from the head of the family, religious leaders, politicians of all persuasions and of course those in business, from small entrepreneur-led firms to huge global corporates. The purpose of this book is to make people, teams and organizations stop and acknowledge that their attitudes, actions and behaviours have a direct and sometimes long-lasting effect on others, and that many people, teams and organizations fail to recognize the leadership role they play.

Everyday leaders have followers: children, families, friends, team members, co-workers, customers, shareholders and electors. Known to them and not. We will offer advice for you, which if acted upon, will make people feel more connected, appreciated, empowered and self-motivated. Yes, you will be leading them but they may not realize, recognize or appreciate the role you have adopted. The everyday leader in the twenty-first century doesn't need to stand up and ask people to follow them; often just setting a strong and visible example will encourage the desired response.

In the book, we aim to take readers on a journey via a series of scenarios, options, advice, and commentaries, each of which explore the full range of leadership challenges that we all encounter every day. But this isn't a 'start at the beginning' and follow a sequential storyline from page one kind of book, as we have tried to design each chapter as a stand-alone offering which you can access directly. So if you want to know more about leading a team, or leading whistleblowing then go straight to the relevant chapter. But before you do, please read Chapters 1 and 15 before going anywhere else. And re-read them regularly so that you can ask those closest to you for a 'progress report' on the changes that you have made (Chapter 1), and so that you can get closer towards the achievement of your dreams (Chapter 15).

Later today and tomorrow you will enjoy many leadership opportunities, but 99 per cent will pass you by unnoticed. Why? Because you don't realize the power you have; the power to change the emotions, activities and behaviours of others. If you need an example, then stop right now and make a call to someone close to you and tell them about the last time they made you happy:

- *'It was really lovely to see you last night, thanks for coming over and having a chat.'*
- *'Thank you helping me with my job application, I couldn't have done it without you. You're the best!'*
- *'John – just a short call to say thank you for your excellent report. I loved it!'*
- *'I couldn't help but notice how well you are looking these days. Whatever you're doing – keep it up!'*

With these calls you have changed the emotional state of the receiver – perhaps only for a few minutes or hours. You have led a positive, albeit temporary, shift in the emotions of those you called. Although we regularly capture and recommend opportunities like these, the main thrust of this book is about introducing and cementing long-lasting and enduring change in others – be they your children, co-workers or bosses, or even by mobilizing your local community. Real, substantive and inspiring change, because leadership can't be called leadership unless it involves change.

This book focuses on how a single individual can create followers to their ideas, opinions, behaviours, beliefs, habits, personal goals and visions of the future. Although three of us have worked together to produce this work, we have decided, with the exception of this Introduction, to use the first person singular style, as it better suits the coaching approach and style that we prefer. Now that we have persuaded you to follow us, let's make a start. We hope you like, and benefit from, what we have to say.

1

Leading Yourself

This is the most important chapter of this book. Without the ability to lead yourself consistently and with assured self-awareness, the likelihood of overcoming other leadership challenges is critically diminished.

When Katie Cutler, aged 23, learned that Alan Barnes had been attacked and mugged by a drug addict outside his home in North-East England she, like the millions of people who became aware of the story, was appalled and disgusted. But unlike the millions of others, Katie decided to do something about it. Although Katie was a young mum struggling with her own problems, she was so moved by the story that she launched a fund to help Alan, and donations quickly poured in. Alan – who was 67, only 4 feet 6 inches tall, registered blind, and who suffered a broken collar bone in the unprovoked attack – found himself at the centre of media attention. With the help of widespread publicity Katie's fund grew to over £330,000, which she handed over to Alan so that he could move home. Katie was dubbed 'the angel of the north' by the press and was awarded the British Empire Medal in recognition of her charitable campaign. Katie is an everyday leader.

The Logic of the 'Inner Voice'

So what differentiated Katie from the millions of others who knew the story? What was the tipping point from sympathy, pity even, to substantive and inspiring action? She led the way where others were more than happy to follow. Katie can't explain it, save to say that her 'inner voice' told her that doing nothing wasn't an option.

Last night I watched a TV programme that showed a hospital ward in which two men were bed ridden. The older man, Joe, aged 92, had been in a road traffic accident, and the younger man, Mohammed, 35, had stopped to help, only for him to be hit by another vehicle leaving him with a number of broken ribs and a host of cuts and bruises. Mohammed led the response to Joe's predicament, suffering painfully in the process.

Katie and Mohammed were selfless and genuinely wanted to help people. The idea that they should take a leadership role was certainly not in their thoughts. But, as it turned out, that is precisely what they did. I don't know how many motorists passed Joe without stopping. I do know that millions didn't help Alan until Katie opened the door and led the way.

I wonder how many of us, myself included, who read about Alan or who saw Joe at the side of the road said to ourselves, 'I want to help but I have other more pressing personal commitments and priorities for my time; I hope things turn out OK for them.' We felt the human connection; we heard our inner voice; we sympathized. But we moved on. In doing so, we put ourselves ahead of those in greater need.

Now that statement seems a little harsh, doesn't it? We're good people after all and normally we are among the first to offer help.

But in these two examples we deferred, leaving others to take the lead.

Katie's and Mohammed's inner voices were insistent and irrefutable – they had no choice but to help. The rest of us, on the other hand, probably heard the same inner voices but the volume was dialled down and messages were drowned out by the shouts of other more immediate concerns and pressing issues. As I shall shortly demonstrate, there is actually something to Katie's inner-voice self-reflection; research is increasingly pointing to the psychological source of this selfless inner voice and the various ways it can be nurtured and encouraged to come to the fore more often.

Leading by example

Observers would say that Katie and Mohammed, by acting on their inner voices, led by example, although they themselves didn't see it that way. And yet everyone else who did nothing led by example as well. How? Let me explain. For those of us who are parents, let's suppose we had our children in the car when Joe's vehicle had broken down at the side of the road, and one of them said, 'Are we going to stop and help, Mummy?' Your response might well have been: 'I'd love to sweetheart, but we have to get to Grandma's and Granddad's by 1 o'clock, so that doesn't leave us much time. We have to press on.' Example set.

If not stopping is your usual response in these situations, then the example you set for your children and anyone around you gets stronger and stronger with every occurrence. I wonder what your children will do in similar circumstances when they are older and they themselves drive past a similar accident. A single fleeting moment when you're not thinking of your responsibilities as an everyday leader will have no lasting impact on your children, of course, but examples where you skirt your greater responsibilities, repeated many times, will. And yet you always have the power, even after years of reinforcing less-than-perfect examples, to erase them and set a different, more caring example, and in this instance, stop to help.

Examples from the world of big business

Leading business executives set the example as well. António Horta Osório, the CEO of Lloyds Banking Group in the UK, set an example in writing by exhorting his tens of thousands of staff to 'lead by example', and then proceeded to undercut his admonition by setting a very bad example when he received widespread adverse publicity alleging that he engaged in an extramarital affair; authenticity and reputation badly damaged at a personal level. At the time, in 2016, he had been married to his wife Anna for 25 years and they had three children together.

After the disclosure he regretted any 'damage done to the group's reputation' caused by allegations over his private life. I think this misses the point completely. Lloyds Bank wasn't damaged at all; he was. Any aura surrounding him became tarnished. Is his alleged cheating always somewhere in the minds of those around him, and those of new business contacts? It would be surprising if it wasn't. He wrote to staff: '*My personal life is obviously a private matter as it is for anyone else.*' His life hasn't been private ever since.

Jeff Fairburn, then Chief Executive of UK housebuilder Persimmon provoked unwanted media headlines when in 2017 he and his senior management team were awarded bonuses which the British newspapers labelled 'preposterous' and 'obscene'. Jeff Fairburn was awarded £110 million; Mike Killoran, finance chief, £86 million; and Dave Jenkinson, group managing director, £48 million. This at a time when house sales were being boosted by the government's 'Help To Buy' scheme and when many of the big housebuilders, including Persimmon, were heavily criticized for the quality of the new homes. Although Jeff has voluntarily given up about a third of that bonus, the furore cost company chairman Nicholas Wrigley and fellow director Jonathan Davie their jobs. Avarice has never been an attractive quality in anyone, let alone the head of a large public company.

Leadership comes with responsibilities. What kind of example were Jeff and his colleagues setting to the staff, customers and shareholders of Persimmon in 2017? Before the end of 2018, it was announced that Jeff would leave the company because of the 'negative impact' of the publicity on the business.

Both Antonio and Jeff are highly competent leaders whose business acumen is widely acknowledged and well regarded, but both made their jobs all the more difficult because of their personal conduct. The conflict between two inner voices, 'do the right thing' or 'do the not-so-right thing, hope there is not too much fallout, and we might get away with it' is a battle that we all must fight, day in day out. Alleged affairs and scandalous bonuses may have passed into legend, but will never to be forgotten by those affected or by the simplest internet search.

Examples from the world of professional sport

Lest we believe that business is especially 'primed' to engender these behaviours, a few examples from the world of sports may disavow us of this view.

Let's start with the case of Phil Mickleson, who at the 2018 US Open Golf Championship gained a potential advantage over his fellow competitors by stopping his ball from rolling off the thirteenth green – an act that has happened before with other golfers but never with Phil. A moment of madness some said, and yet on live television he made no apologies, 'I took advantage of the rules as best I could.' He offered no explanation for stopping the ball and remained unrepentant immediately afterwards. Many commentators criticized his disregard for the spirit and etiquette of the game and his lack of sportsmanship, while some called for him to be disqualified from the tournament. Phil's stature in golf was impossible to over-state, and until 16 June 2018 he enjoyed a reputation for both humility and what appeared to be a genuine friendliness for the fans. All that goodwill tarnished by doing the not-so-right thing in front of hundreds of millions of viewers. One can just imagine someone in the crowd at a future event shouting out, 'Let it come to a stop first Phil!' For many his reputation will never be restored. His error has already passed into legend, never to be expunged. What a shame.

Steve Smith, captain, and David Warner, vice-captain of the Australian Cricket team, were banned from all international and domestic cricket for a year in 2018 after their involvement in a ball tampering scandal during an Australia versus South Africa test match in Cape Town. Bowler Cameron Bancroft admitted to illegally roughing up one side of the cricket ball to make it swing in flight. Steve Smith said the plan was concocted during the lunch break by 'the leadership group'. Back home in Australia, it was painful to watch both Smith and Warner admit their guilt on television, as both broke down, shed tears and apologized for their actions. As Smith admitted, 'I know I will regret this for the rest of my life', Warner said he would, 'do everything I can to be a better person, teammate and role model.'[1]

Those more familiar with the sport of baseball will recognize this as a case of 'scuffing the ball', something a pitcher can do so that the ball moves more sharply as it approaches the plate, thereby fooling even the best batter. Many such cases exist.

In fact, Australian cricketers are more than capable of setting brilliant examples than they are of bad, so please allow me to congratulate Ricky Ponting. In a test match between India and Australia, Ponting set, what is still, a rare example of sportsmanship. Indian batsman Rahul Dravid edged a shot straight to Ponting in the slips who appeared to take the catch. Dravid acknowledged the catch as he turned to walk towards the pavilion. But after only a few steps, he was called back by Ponting who said the ball had touched the ground, and Dravid was therefore 'not out'. Dravid returned to the crease and continued his innings.

Ponting had set a wonderful example. The battle between inner voices was fought and won by doing 'the right thing', even when there may be a short-term disadvantage. Winning in sport should be the end result of developing and executing a successful strategy. How can anyone be proud of triumphs achieved through cheating?

Cheats go into legend, and no matter how reformed they become, the label always dangles over their reputation, like a cheap 'marked for clearance' sticker on unpopular clothes.

Please allow me to repeat one powerful phrase from our earlier discussion that I believe gets to the heart of the matter – 'I know I will regret this for the rest of my life.' One careless moment never to be forgotten.

The science of 'everyday leadership'

Understanding the battle over our 'inner voice(s)'

How good are you at listening to both of your inner voices? Don't answer just yet, while we look at what behavioural research tells us might be at work in the situations we just reviewed.

In the late 1970s a young research economist working at the University of Rochester hosted a dinner party for his colleagues. It was the first major hosting event for him and his partner and they had prepared a roast chicken dinner which was taking a long time to cook. In the meantime they had set out a light snack (roasted cashews) to go along with the wine they were serving. As the chicken cooked and the aroma filled the room, the hunger mounted and more and more nuts were being trotted out to satiate the guests. That is when the hosts decided to save their 'dinner' by removing all the nuts from various trays located around the house. As they did this, something strange began to occur. People started clapping and thanking the guests, even as they reached in one last time to grab a final handful of cashews.

What was going on? To most people they would have chalked up their dinner guests' behaviour to a bad case of the 'munchies'. But this was an economist in a room full of his colleagues; he needed to understand why his guests were simultaneously happy to see the cashews removed, even as they were clearly enjoying the immediate gratification of eating them. The young economist in question was none other than Richard H. Thaler – the 2017 recipient of the Nobel Prize in Economics – and in the course of forty years he has, along with similarly minded colleagues, built up a brand new area of study known as *behavioural economics*, which is the study of economics from a psychological perspective.

At the time, Professor Thaler did not have access to functional Magnetic Resonance Imaging (fMRI) techniques that can in real time map our brains as we engage in various tasks or as we are presented with a set of choices, so instead he created a logical model of what had occurred that essentially described a 'divided self'. One self – the selfish, short-term version – could not say no to the cashews, even as they were knowingly degrading the quality of the dinner to come for both themselves and the host. The second self – the more selfless, rational long-term thinking version – was trying to tame the cashew eater so as to enjoy the meal and to honour the hard work of their hosts.

What we now know of course, is that it was very hard for Professor Thaler's guests – as rational as they were – to properly weigh the (greater) net benefits of the meal to come, whilst they were in a state of hunger and smelling the delicious food wafting through the house. They were in a 'hot mental state' according to researchers, the product of our fast acting limbic system located in the core of our brain that fires up well before our prefrontal neocortex can stir up thoughts and messages that will dissuade us from acting in our immediate self-interest. The prefrontal area of our brain is in charge of 'executive functions' such as long term planning and goal setting, processes that help us make better judgments by more accurately assessing the future consequences of our actions. 'I'm hungry so why can't I eat this bowl of cashews … oh wait I know why because if I eat them now I'll miss out on the better chicken dinner to come. And I won't insult my hosts who spent all-day preparing the dinner.'[2]

The science of the 'first mover' . . . or why most people follow and so few lead

Earlier Katie Cutler set an example that thousands followed. She was a 'first mover'. Let me give you a few other examples.

Baroness Tessa Jowell, an ex-Government minister under Tony Blair's leadership, developed a brain tumour and died in 2018. A few months before her death, she delivered a brilliant speech in the House of Lords about her illness and the treatment she was receiving. At the end of her speech she sat down. Immediately, Lord Bassam of Brighton, who was sitting next to her, started to hear conflicting voices in his head as each battled for dominance. It is obvious when watching him that one voice was telling him to 'stand up' in admiration and the opposing voice telling him to 'maintain decorum and remain seated' as standing and applauding in the House of Lords is frowned upon. Thankfully the battle only lasted for a second as he stood, slightly embarrassed, and in doing so became the 'first mover', leading hundreds of his colleagues in the House to their feet.

Another well-known example, shared widely on social media, occurred at an open air music concert, where one audience member was so moved by the music and just possibly something else as well, that he, alone, starts gyrating. Calling it dancing is to give dancing a bad name, yet hundreds watch him for a few seconds before another man joins him, briefly joining hands with him. Then a third and a fourth join in, etc. Almost immediately, what appears to be the entire audience is up on their feet and dancing. Is it too much of an exaggeration to say that before the 'dancing man' got to his feet, the majority of the audience also *wanted* to get on their feet and dance, but felt too inhibited to do so? A nervous, inner voice saying 'don't embarrass yourself', 'don't make a fool of yourself', until an everyday leader emerged. Hundreds then followed.[3]

These examples are illustrative of two important mechanisms at work: one economic and the other psychological. The economic explanation for why we are reticent to move first, or put another way, why we are more likely to follow someone else's lead, hinges on our inability to accurately estimate the value of a particular 'decision' or to understand the true 'tastes' of others. Economists refer to this behavior as an *informational cascade*, noting that we often use popular behavior as a signal of quality when there is information that we lack or outcomes that we cannot directly observe. This is something encountered many times and in many circumstances. It explains why we line up and wait for a bowl of soup or a pizza at an already popular restaurant but walk by a potentially equally good (but empty) competitor; why we follow the bestseller lists when buying a book at the airport duty free shop but fail to buy a book that is likely better but harder to find; or why we wait and see if a stock 'takes off' before investing ourselves. Or as in the cases reviewed above, why we wait for a 'leader to emerge' from the herd before we follow.

There are also powerful psychological mechanisms at work. In a *reputational cascade* (as distinct from an informational/economic one), herding has more to do with compliance; the notion that subsequent adopters sometimes go along with the decisions of early adopters, not just because late movers think the early movers are 'right', but also because they perceive their own reputation will be damaged if they do not follow. Think of the 100th dancer at the concert or the 100th parliamentarian to stand up, they would have faced the 'ire' of their counterparts had they stayed stuck in their seats. Maybe they would have preferred to stay seated, but at that point they had no choice but to do the 'right thing' if only to preserve their standing amongst their peers.

Are you a 'first mover'? If not, then what is it that holds you back – a lack of knowledge, fear of standing out, or a mix of both? Have a think. The world needs more everyday leaders.

Earlier I suggested that not stopping your vehicle to offer roadside assistance can set an example for your kids. In a study for the Vinci Foundation,[4] it was found that even the driving habits of parents are replicated by their children. From babes in arms to teenagers, your children sit next to you in the vehicle and learn from you. You are their role model, their hero, and if you toot the horn and swear at other drivers you won't be too surprised to learn that your children will probably do the same when they start driving. Observing the speed limit and being courteous to other road users will also set the example.

Even a child's career path can be affected by an off-the-cuff or careless remark. A report published by the *Institution of Engineering & Technology* in 2018[5] has shown that off-the-cuff remarks by parents about their child's mathematics and science homework can have a seriously discouraging effect. If, when asked for help, the parent replies, 'Sorry darling, I'm no good at maths [or physics]', then I wouldn't be surprised if the child's shoulders dropped a little and their inner voice said, 'I might not be any good at maths either.' Contrast a different response, 'Sorry darling, I was never very good at maths but I want to help and maybe we can learn more together.' Discouraging versus encouraging. Be conscious of how your own confidence levels and enthusiasm for specific subjects can influence and shape your children's development from an early age – particularly with the two pillars of reading and maths.

You set the example for everyone around you and it is an extremely strong example, one difficult to break. Many of us don't realize the power we each have to lead the emotions, attitudes and actions of those around us. You lead with everything you say and do. Listen to yourself more carefully. What ideas, attitudes and beliefs have you implanted previously and what will you be signposting today and tomorrow?

What you can do to put everyday leadership into action

You probably remember the film *Forest Gump*, in which Tom Hanks playing the title character runs across the Mojave Desert in America? He collected followers just by running. Nothing else – just running. He sent no texts or emails, in fact there was no promotional work at all, he just 'did it'. You too can set the example by just doing things that are of value but which are not typically seen – taking the family out with a rubbish bag to collect litter in your neighbourhood, for example. Just doing what's right. Others may follow. But it doesn't matter if they don't, you're leading those closest to you by example. Congratulations.

Just as Katie, Mohammed, Antonio, Jeff, Steve, Ricky and Lord Bassam heard their own inner voices and listened to the conflict between opposing courses of action, you too hear them at critical moments. And yet the everyday leader can sometimes be a little hard of hearing, deaf even to ordinary, everyday situations where the moment to influence others flashes past, never to be recovered.

I have just finished reading the brilliant and moving *This is Going To Hurt* by Adam Kay, an ex-junior doctor in England's National Health Service (NHS). He makes the point that he rarely received a simple 'thank you' or 'well done' from anyone of his clinical bosses or those in hospital management's executive positions for his dedication and heroic achievements. How appalling. And the fact that he mentions it in his book testifies to its importance for him. Patients on the other hand were fulsome in their praise of Adam, and extremely grateful for his work. The doctors, nursing and management staff missed perhaps thousands of opportunities to thank Adam. All of us feel the need from time to time to get a little pat on the back, to feel that our work is appreciated.

Many parents, team leaders and government ministers are of course highly conscious of their leadership role, not just with driving habits but with literally everything they do in the presence of their kids, their colleagues and the electorate. How conscious are you? The lesson here: habits are examples, and regardless of whether they are good or bad, they get replicated by our followers. So, stop for a moment and think of yesterday. What examples did you set, both knowingly and unknowingly? How self-aware are you of your habits, both good and not so good? You can lead in all sorts of different ways – positively and negatively. But you and I are setting the example all of the time. Others will follow us. We are the 'dancing man'!

We have discussed leading by example with both action and non-action, but we also lead with our body language. And a smile is the most potent weapon we all have to affect the mood of those around us, but also for complete strangers. Let me give you an example.

Several years ago, I was leaving London on the A41 main arterial road and stopped at traffic lights in an area known as Finchley. Three lanes of stationary vehicles. I looked around at my fellow motorists and in the car next to me was a female driver, who just happened at that precise moment to look at me. Our eyes met, and unusually for me, and a little nervously, I smiled. She returned my smile. My heart jumped in a brief moment of joy before the traffic lights changed and we were off. I led with body language and she responded. Nothing else happened – this isn't the start of a romantic interlude – but I quote it as an example of how we can lead the emotions of others. I have tried it at other times and with different drivers and can confirm that it works more often than not; though sometimes the odd trucker does not return the gesture as sent, but instead uses a different gesture in reply. Regardless, try it for yourself, and don't wait for others to initiate the smile – lead the exchange yourself.

In their book *Connected: The Surprising Power of Our Social Networks and How They Shape Our Lives*, two medical researchers Nicholas A. Christakis and James H. Fowler report on a startling set of findings from the social network literature: things that we never thought of as contagious (i.e. obesity, loneliness, smoking) had powerful social contagion effects. And the connections did not even appear to be direct, but rather could be influenced by people that you had never even met. In their words:

> as we began to think about the idea that people are connected in vast social networks, we realized that social influence does not end

> with the people we know. If we affect our friends, and they affect their friends, then our actions can potentially affect people we have never met. We began by studying various health effects. We discovered that if your friend's friend's friend gained weight, you gained weight. We discovered that if your friend's friend's friend stopped smoking, you stopped smoking. And we discovered that if your friend's friend's friend became happy, you became happy.

Now imagine what someone in great authority could do armed with this knowledge of social contagion; just by virtue of their public behaviour they could affect millions of people, either positively or negatively. We don't have to look too far to find an answer. Apparently Donald Trump gets bored easily. His listeners too, I guess. No issue there, except that when in public view, he disrespects those speaking by crossing his arms, adopting a hangdog look, and swivelling in his chair. His body language is saying, 'I'm as bored as hell and want to be somewhere else'. What kind of example is he setting? He could have chosen a different pose, leaning forward, engaging eye contact with the speaker and nodding occasionally. Leading dialogue, discussion and openness instead of shutting it down.

How can you be a better wife, husband, brother, sister, parent, daughter, son, grandchild, work buddy, team leader or senior executive? Best-selling author Marshall Goldsmith recommends asking the question outright, for example, 'Sweetheart, how can I be a better husband?' After reading this in one of Marshall's works, I asked my wife the exact same question. Her reply? 'Well, you can start by putting the toilet seat down every time after you pee.' I took the challenge seriously, but it took me a year to accomplish the task consistently.

My reward? 'Good.' To be honest I'd expected a lot more – an extra date night perhaps or a flypast by the Red Arrows. But now, three years later I'm still putting the seat down. A new habit. Onwards and upwards.

So next time you grab the door handle of your car to get out, either to go shopping or into your office, pause for a millisecond and set the example. People are watching you for clues – friendly, hostile, distant, approachable, confident, happy, sad or troubled. Whatever your actual mood, consider transmitting a positive, upbeat demeanour with your body language. The point is others will be affected even if you can't read them.

Question: By email and through direct questioning, ask your friends, family and colleagues, what they believe are your good habits and your bad ones. Tell them that you are completing an exercise to prepare yourself for more responsibility in the way you comport yourself and need their help to identify the areas where you should focus your efforts. Ask them to be totally honest and respond within seven days.

I'm told this is where I set a good example, and these are my good habits	I'm told this is where I could set a better example, and these are my less good habits

The Everyday Leader trusts their inner voice, focusing not on immediate personal gains but on long-term benefits and is mentally prepared to 'go first' when no one else is prepared to act.
The Everyday Leader regularly seeks input from others about their words, body language and actions and, like an auditor examining a set of accounts, spots where improvements could be made.
The Everyday Leader doesn't allow their growing self-confidence inadvertently to make statements or act in a way which doesn't fully recognize the negative impact they may have on the feelings of others. Likewise, they recognize that through their selfless words and actions, they positively influence not only those around them, but also those far removed.

2

Leading by listening

This chapter looks at gathering intelligence about the world you inhabit, both as a private citizen and as someone working in an organization (commercial or not-for-profit) and using that intelligence to draw a conclusion and shape a response.

Erin Brockovich is an American legal clerk and environmental activist, who, despite her lack of formal education in law, was instrumental in building a case against the Pacific Gas and Electric Company of California in 1993. The case alleged contamination of drinking water with hexavalent chromium in the southern Californian town of Hinkley. And it all started when Erin was organizing papers on a pro bono real estate case. She found medical records that shocked her, and that eventually would explode into the largest direct action lawsuit in US history. Hollywood came knocking on Erin's door and Julia Roberts represented her in a blockbuster movie. Erin not only put two and two together and made four, but then showed enormous determination and persistence to lead a community response. Good observation and action from Erin, but how many others missed the same clues? Why were they were not tuned in to listen in on the same signals that she did?

Ask yourself if you are too busy to watch and listen, too obsessed with your personal to-do-list to see perhaps more important problems or opportunities accumulating at your door.

What happens when we fail to listen?

People watching is a popular pastime. Grab a coffee outside a café on a busy street and observe those who pass. Where are they from? What sort of clothes are they wearing? Where might they be going? Is that their partner with them or is it just a friend? People love this stuff.

I wonder what people think when I walk past. What do you think they say about you as you stroll by? Everyone is an expert witness. We notice things. Erin noticed something, and then did something about it – leading by listening, watching and acting.

Abused children and why no one in authority took action

Contrast Erin's response after spotting something wrong, with the leadership (or lack thereof) of the authorities in Rotherham, England for more than two decades. Organized child sexual abuse continued virtually unchallenged in the northern English town after it was first recorded in the early 1990s.Taxis were used to pick up children from schools and care homes and they were then subjected to the most horrific exploitation. Front-line care home managers reported these activities and even offered the names of some of the men involved.

Those in authority refused to acknowledge the complaints and warnings. The front-line workers at the time took it no further. In short, nothing happened.

The police and council managers had seen, but not noticed; heard, but not listened. Were they deliberately pretending to be blind and deaf? Either way, they took no action. Executives and senior managers of agencies directed to protect vulnerable youth might have occupied positions of *authority*, but showed woefully inadequate *leadership*. That's because authority and leadership are not the same thing. Erin Brockovich, as a law clerk had no formal authority, but demonstrated plenty of leadership in her struggle to hold the polluters in her community to account. The Chief Executive of Rotherham Council, the director of the Council's children's services, and the police and crime commissioner did not. In the end they were all forced to resign in shame.[1]

In early 2018, Larry Nasser, the former US Gymnastics doctor, was sentenced to a maximum 170 years behind bars for sex crimes against girl gymnasts. Prosecutor, Angela Povilaitis, read a statement summarizing how Nassar had escaped prosecution for so long, and then asked, 'What does it say about our society when victims do come forward and they are automatically met with scepticism and doubt, treated as liars until proven true?' She turned to the dozens of Nassar's accusers in the back of the courtroom, her voice breaking with emotion, and thanked them for coming forward. 'We have seen the worst of humanity and the best in the last couple of days ... how one voice can start a movement, how a reckoning can deliver justice,' she said.

Learning from the horrible cases of abuse and institutional inaction

Good people often feel inhibited or constrained from doing something about a particular issue. Are you, and others like you, being shouted down by those with more authority or power? Are you fearful of losing your job and therefore much needed income? Are you afraid of retribution? Or are you simply afraid to act alone?

The story of April Bloomfield, a Michelin-starred chef working out of the now infamous Spotted Pig restaurant in New York City, illustrates all of the above.[2] In an instant she watched her world break apart. In a recent interview with the *New York Times* she said that 'she now understands that her silence contributed to the sexual and emotional harassment of workers she should have protected'. It turns out that her business partner, a man named Ken Freidman, was a serial abuser and harasser of his employees. Most of his victims were young and all of them female. In her own recounting of events, Chef Bloomfield recalled 'being terrified of being branded a failure in the restaurant industry, and was convinced that Mr Freidman had the power to make that happen'.

But even when Mr Freidman stepped away from all business operations amid the controversy, she still kept quiet. It turns out her lawyers advised silence while the breakup of the restaurant group (they owned other restaurants in New York and California) was completed.

In Chapter 1 we looked at the long line of social-psychological research demonstrating the power of conformity – why we wait for a pizza at a busy restaurant and pass by a similar restaurant with few customers – which prevents individuals from acting on their own accord and in ways that defy group behaviour. If no one acts in the face of terrible information, then the rest of us are less likely to act as well, especially if we are in a position that lacks authority.

So, do the inner voices of those aware of crimes and other forms of wrong-doing hear themselves thinking: Is it my responsibility to raise this issue, to report it? But everyone seems to be aware of it happening, even people at higher levels and yet nothing is done to stop it? Is it my place? Should I be the one to report this?

The everyday leader is definitely challenged in these situations and deserves some sympathy. In Chapter 13 we will discuss whistle-blowing and the kind of leadership that needs to emerge in such difficult circumstances.

Noticing what you see, listening to what you hear and then taking action

What we always have to keep in mind is that one voice *can* make a difference. As we saw with the example of Katie Cutler in Chapter 1, you too can start a movement – be it a national cause or a more local version. The story of the late Ian Kiernan is another example.[3]

In 1987, during a global yacht race, Mr Kiernan set an Australian record for solo circumnavigation. It was during that race that he became aware of, and appalled by, the trash he saw in the Sargasso Sea, a region of the Atlantic Ocean where four currents converge. Ian was certainly not the only sailor to have observed such waste, but he was the first to take notice and act. He was outraged and according to Kim McKay, a close friend and the director of the Australian Museum, 'When he returned to Sydney he walked into my office and said, "I think we need to organize a cleanup."'

Together they gathered a small group of friends to volunteer and clean up Sydney Harbour, which unlike today, was an outlet for the city's raw sewage and was strewn with everything from rusted car bodies to cigarette butts. It was Sunday 8 January 1989. Ian and Kim expected a few hundred people to help (remember this was the era before mobile phones, social media and the internet). Instead 40,000 people showed up. 'Clean Up Australia' was founded the following year and in 1993 'Clean Up the World' expanded the movement globally, and today millions of volunteers in more than 100 countries participate in clean-up efforts annually. In a statement after Ian's funeral in 2018, Australia's Prime Minister Scott Morrison observed that Ian's passion for the oceans 'struck a real chord ... The thing that ... Ian did most was just tap us all on the shoulder and say, "Hey, we've got to take care of this."'

So, if after noticing that something needs fixing, your first instinct is to enlist some like-minded people around you – much like Ian Kiernan did when he stormed into his friend's office – then do so. And if it helps, pin this well-known quote by Margaret Mead to your fridge door so you can be reminded of it every morning: 'Never doubt that a small group of thoughtful, committed citizens can change the world; indeed, it's the only thing that ever has.'

Mead, as it turns out, was a cultural anthropologist, who spent most of her professional career observing cultures in the South

Pacific and drawing conclusions about human behaviour.[4] Like Mead you need to watch, listen and observe. Have you noticed that your child is more subdued of late, your partner is spending less time at the local gym and more time in front of the TV watching sports, one of your parents is losing weight, or that your boss is dressing differently? Have you noticed that one of your children is more motivated to go to school, your partner is more affectionate with you, one of your parents is now walking without the aid of a walker, or that your boss is asking your opinion more often? Changes in the behaviour of others have causes. It would be good to know what they are because you can then fashion an appropriate response. The world around you is changing every second. Opportunities and threats are ever present.

The everyday leader is always alert and interested in what is going on around them. They have a sensitive radar, their eyes and ears are constantly gathering and interpreting a range of emotions, ideas, statistics and events far and wide. But more – the everyday leader looks out, not in. All too often we can become too self-focused, self-centred, that we are in danger of missing the signals that others are transmitting. Yes, it's quite natural to focus on the things that we have to do, our to-do-list, our responsibilities, our duties even. And yes, it's difficult to step back and try to take in the bigger picture when we have so much to do, but our power to influence and to shape the future is substantially enhanced when we do.

You don't need the *Sun* newspaper, the *Washington Post* or the *Financial Times* to listen and observe. You don't need the *Harvard Business Review or McKinsey Quarterly* to understand a particular problem at work. But you do need to notice and not just see; to listen and not just hear. There are important problems in need of resolving all around you; the everyday leader does not shy away from these. You may already be aware of one or two of them in your local religious congregation; your child's sports club; the local care home. Or maybe there is something at work that has caught your attention and suspicion? You are almost certainly not alone.

Sorry if this sounds a little harsh, but are you using the excuse that you are simply 'too busy to do the right thing'? When future headlines scream, will you have played a part?

Two hypothetical scenarios, one optimal course of action

When we listen and observe we get closer to the nature of things. We get to the root cause. And without understanding the root causes of events, we are in danger of reacting to symptoms.

Let's take two scenarios that present everyday leadership challenges at home: Your child is suddenly more subdued, your partner suddenly more affectionate – what is the reason for this?

Your child is more subdued. 'Why?' you ask, but get the brush off – 'Nah, everything's fine, just got a lot of homework to do.' This could be true, but it could be a deflection away from a more deep-seated problem. You smile, 'OK, Son, good luck with it.' But your radar remains active over the next few days, desperately seeking any further mood changes. You think back to your own childhood, and those now trivial and insignificant worries that at the time seemed gigantic and all-consuming; bullying (in person or, these days, on social media), the loss of a favourite friend to a rival group, an embarrassing moment with one of the teachers, and so on.

How will you tease the real reason(s) out of your child and into the open, and then offer your advice?

I recommend that you consider seizing an appropriate moment while watching a television programme together, or when reading a story in the local papers or on social media and using it to confess to your own childhood worries. Children can carry a lot of guilt about what is happening around them; feeling somehow complicit in the situation or wrong-doing. Open up about your own feelings as a child.

Looking back to when I was growing up, bullying was more the norm than not. Thankfully today, there is a much more robust and focused intolerance of abuse in whatever form. Recently my granddaughter started getting headaches at school, which disappeared after she was collected and returned home. Her mother discovered that she and her friend were being teased incessantly by a small group of boys. The reaction of the school teachers and the parents of the abusers was immediate and strong, and this teasing stopped.

Your children are mini-versions of you and they are going through the same stuff that you went through. Tell them how you felt as a child and the inner voices that you heard at the time – especially the ones that you never confessed to. As an adult you now better understand the root causes of the threats and problems you faced as a child. And if you have never opened up about your experiences, then consider doing so; share them at the side of your child's bed last thing at night. That's everyday leadership.

Let's switch gears and look at scenario number two: your partner becomes noticeably more affectionate. A welcome, if unexpected change, or a handicap to the timely completion of items on your to-do-list. Whatever the result, what do you do? Do you call your partner up on it, or let it pass without comment? Is it a temporary change to your relationship or a more permanent one? Is it a symptom? If so, what might be the possible root cause? Ask yourself what the everyday leader would do.

To make it easier, let's assume that one of your best friends raises this exact same issue and asks for your help. How would you lead him or her through their confusing set of emotions? Let's look at some of the more – and less – likely reasons:

Possible cause	**Yes/No**
Your partner started a new yoga or meditation class	
Their relief at a threat to the family not materializing	
A close friend decides to split from their partner	
A secret crush they had on another person has evaporated	
They recently read a new book or watched a TV programme about relationships	
They closed down a secret affair	
The intensity of your animal magnetism has become overwhelmingly irresistible	
Hormonal changes	
You have come into a lot of money	

Feel free to add a couple more from your own experiences. After listing the possible causes, let's draw up a few options and likely outcomes.

- ***Option 1: 'Ask right away without first listening and observing.'*** You recommend that your friend bring up the subject with their partner right away, and they do. 'I love these extra embraces that I'm getting, but I don't really understand why I'm getting them.' When you next meet up with your friend, they report their partner's response: 'Are you complaining? Can't I give you a hug now and again? Fine, if you don't like it I'll stop.' That could have gone better.
- ***Option 2 'Listen and Learn.'*** You recommend that your friend keeps quiet for a little while, enjoys the new moments, perhaps responding in kind even, but keeps in mind the list you created together, gradually ticking off the non-starters. When you next meet up, they report that their spouse revealed over dinner that a close friend had a serious accident and is now more determined to live in the moment and enjoy every day as their last. Your friend thinks it has rubbed off on their partner. By listening and observing, the underlying reason was revealed and a better outcome procured.

Of course there is always Option 3 – do nothing. But that's not for the everyday leader, is it?

Real-life examples of leading by listening

Listening in the world of sport

Sports coaches have to listen and observe – it's their job. They talk about muscle memory. In golf, for example, even the top players in the world have their coaches with them on the practice grounds during important matches. Both player and coach know that correct golf swings, repeated over and over create a muscle memory model that may endure for the following few hours. And yet the next day they are both back on the practice ground repeating the repeats, because they know they can't rely on yesterday for their today.

So it is for the everyday leader. They know, as they're getting washed and dressed, that not only must they set the right example for those around them, but they must also be acutely aware of the words, attitudes, behaviours and demeanours of others. They must listen, observe and respond appropriately. Some everyday leaders have a list of people that they will contact during each day, if not in person, then by telephone or email: family members; community members; and people at work. How effective are you at maintaining your personal and professional networks?

Listening in the world of business

To be effective, people in business have to listen to and observe every little nuance within their own industry and within their own company. When Tony Ryan and Michael O'Leary got together and launched Ryanair on the same low-cost model that US airline Southwest had pioneered, their low prices started a price war that has affected all airlines in Europe, and continues to this day. What a wonderful example of leadership. Tony and Michael watched, listened and microscopically examined the then industry model and decided to break it apart. They have led and continue to lead the airline industry with innovations that others have been forced to copy.

Scanning your environment for clues to what's going on

Tony and Michael probably never used the analytic model PESTLE, but they may have instinctively. The acronym represents a series of external factors that should be examined and analysed before important decisions are made: politics, economics, social forces, technological changes, legal changes and the environment. To be sure, new economy founders like Larry Page and Sergey Brin at Google; Jeff Bezos at Amazon; or Mark Zuckerberg at Facebook were likely less interested in assessing their environment and more keen on replacing existing business models with entirely new ones before launching their respective enterprises. But before you skip ahead, thinking that PESTLE is no longer applicable in today's dynamic economy and may not apply to you as an individual, consider this:

- *Political forces* – if you're a Brit and have relatives in Europe with different nationalities then perhaps you could obtain dual nationality as insurance against the Brexit changes.

- *Economic factors* – are you working in an expanding industry with a glowing future? If not and it's slowly dying then perhaps it's time to retrain ahead of the majority.
- *Social forces* – is the unrelenting drive for profit in a capitalist society suiting you and yours, or is the appeal for a more back-to-basics simple existence becoming more attractive? In what social environment do you want to raise your family?
- *Technological change* – soon we will have driverless cars, vans, trucks and planes. Robots will diagnose our illnesses and perform surgery. Will your job be given up to a robot? If so, what re-training are you considering?
- *Legal developments* – will planned future changes to regulations in consumer protection, health and safety, tax or money laundering have an impact on your circumstances?
- *The environment* – will growing levels of air and water pollution and a warming climate cause you to re-think your geographic location at some point?

Most of us would do well to pause once in a while and examine the larger context under which we live and operate on a daily basis. We all look before we walk across the street and we listen to a question before providing an answer. And come to think of it, a little more listening and environmental scanning by business leaders like Mark Zuckerberg may have prevented the 'tone deaf' responses to allegations of data breaches and political meddling that occurred on Facebook during the Brexit referendum and the American presidential election. It would also have saved the company billions of dollars of lost market value.

Everyday leaders don't rely on their yesterdays to get them through their todays. And they carry their responsibilities with joy as they know they are making a difference. If you're refreshing your everyday leadership or just starting out as a conscious everyday leader, then try to emulate the habits of medal-winning swimmers who know that they have to swim more lengths than those who finish behind them, and those successful potters who know they have to throw more clay than hobbyists. Everyday leadership is a state of mind that requires daily reactivation and re-energizing. But just like successful swimmers and potters, it becomes easier the more often you do it. You will make terrific progress early on, but then just like dieters and fitnessers, your improvements will plateau. At that point it might be time to think about taking on a personal coach.

On a more serious note, some of the examples of inaction and poor leadership reviewed in this chapter, especially those of abuse gone unchecked, may have been difficult to read. But the results needn't have been as bad if at least a few good people had decided to listen and to take note of what was going on around them. That would have been everyday leadership in action. Fortunately we also reviewed examples of people who did not sit still or remained quiet. Instead they allowed the full scope of what was happening around them to sink in. By doing so, they began to understand the causes and worked to find solutions.

Question. Think about how you gain knowledge and insight, and through what media? Then think about your reaction to this learning. What did you do as a result, and what could you have done?

I access these information sources to keep up to date with what's going on in my world and the world	I apply the knowledge I acquire to help me influence, motivate and persuade others to help me with these goals and priorities

The Everyday Leader pays more attention to those with opposing views and really listens to what they are saying in order to better understand the world as it truly is and not as she wishes it to be.
The Everyday Leader doesn't build ever stronger relationships with like-minded people but extends relationships to those with different views.
The Everyday Leader watches and learns, listens and then acts with purpose and resolve.
The Everyday Leader enlists a few devoted followers before taking action and starting a movement.

3

Leading your team

This chapter contrasts two different styles of leadership, 'leading by demands and encouragement' and 'leading by letting go'. As a leader of people both at home and at work, you know that no one single leadership style works for everyone. You have to be flexible and adaptable, switching between two or more styles as the occasion, person or group demands, and blending them in various combinations to suit particular circumstances. But before we take a look at examples of both approaches, here are some questions for you as an everyday leader of people:

1. Why does your team exist, or put another way, what is its purpose?
2. How successful is it?
3. What is your vision for the team?
4. What do your team members want from you as their leader?
5. Have you studied the input, output and process data? What does it reveal?
6. How would you describe the team culture?
7. What is the team's reputation?

8 Who are your star performers and your weakest links?

9 How would you describe the dynamics within the team?

10 Do the roles and responsibilities of each team member play to their strengths?

11 What is it exactly that you, the leader, bring to the table?

12 What are the top three things you have learned as a team leader?

My hunch is that you probably interpreted the above questions as a leader at work, but now I want you to look at them again from a parent's perspective within the family. For the first question, you may decide that your family exists as a shelter; a refuge; a place of safety and comfort; a place of emotional support; providing succour to young and elderly. It would be interesting if, at some point, you compared your answers with those of the rest of the family and discussed their various responses.

I don't think there's a better job on the planet than being a parent. And as parental leaders we all know (or will soon learn) that 'leading by demands and encouragement' eventually has to give way to 'leading by letting go'.

One family's leadership journey

Geoff Whitington, 63, was overweight, diabetic and on the verge of losing a leg to the disease. Geoff knew that his lifestyle was killing him, and yet he was prepared to die rather than make changes. Once, when Geoff was in hospital, the diabetic in the next bed was being prepared for an operation to amputate his foot. Geoff was shocked, and then realized that perhaps he should get his own life in order before he found himself in a similar or even worse situation.

Turning around his health would mean changing his habits of poor food choices and no exercise. So in 2013 his sons, Anthony and Ian, decided to make a project of fixing their dad's ill health, and in that moment they became leaders of the family. Geoff became their child. This role reversal happens to all of us at some point.

The sons knew that 'leading by letting go' was not an option, as Geoff was unable to remedy the situation by himself; he point blank refused to do the things that were necessary. He needed help. This was a very difficult challenge for his sons. They intervened, but Geoff resisted with a passion for many weeks and months. 'I'm not doing it. I'm telling you, I'm not doing it!' Facing his almost insurmountable stubbornness, and frequent tears, Anthony and Ian acknowledged they were in for a long haul.

The sons forced their dad to confront the brutal facts of his medical condition and prospects, whilst gently and persistently encouraging small step changes. The brothers committed to sticking with their dad, and agreed that anything they asked him to do, they would do themselves. This included regimes for fitness, nutrition and mind-set. It involved constant blood sugar monitoring, stress reduction practices, time commitment and dedication.

Over the course of the following 12 months, not only did Geoff reverse his Type 2 diabetes and come off his medications for high blood pressure and high cholesterol, both Anthony and Ian also lost weight, became fitter and vastly improved their own health along the way. More importantly, the whole family grew much closer.

Relationships improved and time together was prioritized in a way that hadn't been before. Anthony and Ian are everyday leaders. They accepted the challenge of leading someone who had been their leader for many years and they made big positive changes. Their efforts led not only their dad but others who heard about their story to follow their example. They filmed the whole uplifting journey and it's available at www.fixingdad.com.

Here are the key takeaways from the story of Geoff and his two sons:

1. Confront the brutal facts, however painful.
2. Don't ask for changes that you are not prepared to make.
3. Join the subject in their world and feel their pain.
4. Reinforce progress by charting small step gains.
5. Regularly look back at discarded old habits, and reward their loss.
6. Re-prioritize your commitments to give the subject a lot of your time and attention.

For the everyday leader, trying to lead a close family member away from poor choices, from a sedentary lifestyle, and from any type of addiction is probably the toughest challenge of all. Because you love them so much, you can see close up just how much the change is hurting them. They will feel genuine pain during the process, and because of the strong emotional bond you have with them, you will feel the same pain. This may tempt you to ease off, to let the recovery milestones slide a little further out. But before you start giving in, put your leadership hat on and focus on the ultimate goal. This will mean doing your research as there is plenty of help available for you via books, social media and professional counselling. I wonder how many people will be disadvantaged today because they do not have an everyday leader in their lives like you, close by to help them? As an aside, it was recently revealed that an average of 120 amputations occur every day in the UK because of diabetes. Let's hope that people are motivated by Geoff's story, and this book, to bring that number down to zero.

Contrasting leadership styles: the case of the orchestra conductor

Alternating between demands and encouragement would apply to all everyday leaders at home, who know when to switch between the two. So it is in the community and at work. The constant use of threats or rewards loses potency over time. Sticks should be avoided and carrots used only occasionally.

One day, when looking through the Sunday papers in print or online, you spot an opportunity to go and see a famous orchestra play one of your favourite pieces of music. You buy tickets for the family. You and perhaps a thousand other music-lovers settle into your seats, as a feeling of anticipation and excitement pervades the auditorium. The conductor walks on, raises her baton and you are treated to a wonderful performance. Your heart sings and cries of emotion get stuck in your throat.

The next day you start thinking about the role of a conductor and how they can assemble such a wonderful team of international musicians and create such a brilliant performance. After all, the conductor is the leader of the orchestra, just like a project team leader would assemble their group of employees at work, or indeed as the CEO of a multi-national organization would recruit the best talent. How do they achieve such successful outcomes? You fire up the internet and search the Wikipedia entry on orchestra conductors to get a preliminary answer to your question. The entry defines 'the primary responsibilities of the conductor are to unify performers, set the tempo, execute clear preparations and beats, listen critically and shape the sound of the ensemble, and to control the interpretation and pacing of the music.'

That's everyday leadership in a nutshell, isn't it? For people at work; for football coaches; for politicians; and for you and me. The size of the team is irrelevant. The skills involved in leading are incredibly similar for all, but crucially, any one of a number of different styles can be employed to satisfy a particular group (family, concert audiences, football supporters, work colleagues, shareholders, etc.). Moreover, styles can (and should be allowed to) change even during a performance, project, game, or in a given accounting period.

And yet it's true that leaders do have a preferred style. Contrast Herbert von Karajan and Leonard Bernstein, for example. Karajan, an Austrian, was the principal conductor of the Berlin Philharmonic for over 30 years and widely acclaimed as one of the greatest conductors of the twentieth century. It is said that his technique was highly controlled, conducting sometimes with his eyes closed. Leonard Bernstein, an American, was a brilliant conductor of the New York Philharmonic, a composer, author and master story-teller. Bernstein's technique was highly demonstrative, with expressive facial gestures.

His movement and energy was contagious, his smile an adoration of what he heard. Karajan could conduct for hours without moving his feet, while Bernstein would often leap into the air at the emotional climax of a symphony. Different leadership styles but both incredibly effective. Karajan would find it impossible to imitate Bernstein and vice versa.

As an everyday leader you shouldn't try to copy the Karajans or Bernsteins in your world, or anyone else that you admire for that matter. The lesson to be learned from the case of the orchestra conductors is that you should be true to yourself. You know who you are, and so do those around you. This book isn't recommending one style over another, but rather asks you to self-analyse and situate yourself along that spectrum (i.e., from control and encouraging to loose and inspirational), so as to maximize the leadership talent and effectiveness of the real you.

And remember that just as Karajan and Bernstein told stories in sound and movement, so do you. Research has shown that the tone of your voice and your body language are often better at communicating than the words you choose, often hurriedly.

The generalizability of team leadership

Now if pop music culture is more your scene, or garage or grime, take heart. They are the same stories of sound but told in different languages. All performances lead their audiences to a level of empathy and appreciation that encourages them to sing along – the audience and artist as one. And sometimes the performing artists do something incredible. They stop playing and stop singing, leaving the audience to sing, unaccompanied, by themselves. That's leadership.

When your family agreed to accompany you to the concert, you agreed to take them to a subsequent football match as their treat. During the game, as you observe the managers at the side of the pitch, you start to wonder if leading a football team is any different to leading an orchestra. One of the managers, the home team, has sat throughout the entire game, only once getting up and that was at halftime to enter back into the dressing room. The other manager, the visiting team, hasn't sat down once, gesturing to his players, yelling at the officials and generally working as hard on the sidelines as some of his actual players on the pitch!

So you reframe the conductor's job in your head: 'the primary responsibilities of the conductor (football coach) are to unify performers (link defenders, midfield and strikers into a pattern of play), set the tempo, execute clear preparations and beats (fitness, nutrition and skill training programmes), listen critically and shape the sound of the ensemble (the game plan, tactics and pattern of play), and to control the interpretation and pacing of the music (making substitutions to change the shape and/or pace of the game).'

Look back to the first responsibility of the conductor 'to unify performers'. Irrespective of race, religion, sexual orientation, disability, gender, age, income or social class, the everyday leader's job is to unify; to cement; to bond together a group of people who may know and love one another (family), or perhaps have never met and never will in person, or have been brought together for a work project. That's quite a challenge.

Unity through purpose, motivation through inspiration

So how would you unify your team? How do you get a, perhaps disparate, group of individuals, strangers to each other, to willingly sign up and commit to achieving a set goal, aim or objective?

Well, for a start, they will only do what you ask with intensity and commitment if they believe that the achievement of the goal will do good for some group (for people), for some 'thing' (for the environment), or for some outcome (for more equality, greater fairness etc.). The aim has to inspire. It has to inspire the team members to subordinate their own interests, prejudices and tolerances, and cooperate for the common good. Not an easy task for the everyday leader. And so you will never inspire team members with an objective that is not worthwhile and to which they feel no emotional connection, e.g. 'let's strive for an extra 10 per cent over last year's revenue'. Who cares?

One often hears the phrase, 'We have to go the extra mile'. Why? What if, instead, you were told: 'Our job is to make seniors feel less lonely.' Brilliant! Sign me up for duty.

There is in fact a solid body of motivational research, going back decades to the pioneering work of Frederick Herzberg and others, which demonstrates that the 'purpose' motive is by far one of the strongest reasons for doing what we do. Often times, for little or no pay, we work on things intensely. The reason is that as human beings we have a strong desire to feel that we are making a difference and having an impact. In situations where the purpose motive is absent, it is near impossible to ask people to go above and beyond the call of duty. In fact, it is here where complicated managerial incentive and compensation systems often have to emerge, or worse, threats and coercion, to get people to do what they do.

In one well-known study by Wharton business school professor Adam Grant, which examined whether infusing a task with purpose can motivate high performance, the results were striking.[1]

In the experiment he took paid employees at a public university's call centre that were phoning potential donors to the school. For anyone who has tried cold calling people for money, you know it can be a tough task. Employees don't get paid much and suffer frequent rejections from people unhappy about getting calls during the football game. Turnover is high and morale is often low. So how do you motivate workers to stay on the phone and bring in the donations?

One relatively easy answer, if you believe in the power of incentives, is that you pay them more for each donation received. Or, using the logic of purposeful motivation, you might consider introducing the callers to someone who was helped by those donations.

To test whether the purpose motive worked or not, in the actual experiment some of these employees heard stories from other employees describing what they perceived were the personal benefits of the job, including financial benefits and the development of skills and knowledge (Grant called this the Personal Benefit condition). However, another set of employees heard stories from the beneficiaries of the fundraising organization, who described how the scholarships they obtained from the organization had a positive impact on their lives (Grant called this the Task Significance condition). Finally, there was a third group of employees that did not read any stories (Control condition). Grant was able to obtain the number of pledges earned as well as the amount of donation money obtained by the callers both one week prior to the study and one month afterwards.

So what were the results? Employees in the Personal Benefit and Control groups secured the same number of pledges and raised the same amount of money as they had before the intervention. But the callers who had interacted with the scholarship students spent more than twice as many minutes on the phone than either the 'personal benefit' or 'control groups', obtained more than twice the number of weekly pledges (from an average of 9 to an average of 23) and brought in vastly more money: a weekly average of $503.22, compared to just $185.94 for the other two groups.

Grant has devoted significant chunks of his professional career to examining what motivates workers in settings that range from call centres and mail-order pharmacies to swimming pool lifeguard squads. In all these situations, Grant says, employees who know how their work has a meaningful, positive impact on others are not just happier than those who don't; they are vastly more productive, too.

So let me ask you. Have you managed to unify your team to a common purpose? Your family (to abandon single-use plastic by 2020); your local community (to lobby for improvement to local roadworks that will reduce accidents); your work colleagues (to build an app that brings lonely senior citizens together with shared interests)?

A commitment to 'holistic' team success

Anecdotal reports suggest that top teams have a winning mentality. I'm not going to argue with that, but I don't believe that winning is the objective, just as profit is not the objective for businesses.

Winning and profit are the results, the outcome, of a team cemented and bound together to do good; to tackle the most demanding goals with an unbending determination to succeed against the odds. And it reflects the level of cooperation and coordinated efforts between various functional teams: First team squad, youth academy, physios, ground-staff, nutritionists and chefs, media professionals, fitness and player coaches, sales, marketing, operations, manufacturing, finance, human resources, information and communication technology, etc.

And there are two essential levels of teamwork needed: the enthusiastic and unified cooperation between people in their own team (e.g., ground-staff); and the enthusiastic cooperation between teams (e.g. marketing and IT). I believe that it's the levels of unification and whole-hearted commitment in the entire organization, rather than the purchase of star performers, that separates the trophy winners from the runners-up. There is again evidence which backs this up.

In a published study that one of us conducted of baseball team performance going back to the 1920s, we asked the question, 'Does the superstar model of team building actually work or does having a more even distribution of talent improve team performance?'[2]

We were inspired to ask such a question after reading a quote from one of the most successful coaches in NBA league history, Phil Jackson, who had this to say about team success:

> The real reason the [Chicago] Bulls won six NBA championships in nine years is that we plugged into the power of oneness instead

> of the power of one man. Sure, we had Michael Jordan, and you have to credit his talent. But at the other end of the spectrum, if players 9, 10, 11, and 12 are unhappy because Michael takes twenty-five shots a game, their negativity is going to undermine everything. It doesn't matter how good individual players are – they can't compete with a team that is awake and aware and trusts each other. People don't understand that.[3]

As reflected by Jackson's observation of why the Chicago Bulls were so successful over so many years, one of the key determinants was having the best player at the time, Michael Jordan, on the team. But equally as important was team chemistry: how the players, irrespective of their individual abilities, worked together. As a leader and assembler of teams, one way of ensuring team chemistry is by being as attentive to the distribution of talent as to the overall average. Rather than simply hiring the best individuals that money can buy, the best managers attempt to maximize joint performance by recruiting, assembling and motivating the best group of workers possible. This is true whether the manager oversees the sales force of a New Jersey real estate office, runs the shop floor of a manufacturing plant in Shanghai or coaches from the sidelines of a football pitch in Leeds.

What did the actual results show for baseball? Controlling for a team's average level of ability, the study found that a certain degree of star power leads to greater team success; however, too much star power, as measured by the difference in ability between the team's top five players versus its bottom five, is bad. In short, while individual skill is key to increasing production, assembling a well-balanced team is an equal, if not more important, consideration over the long run.

Successful coaches, like all good leaders, assemble the right group of players so that they can put the person into the role, not the role into the person. A striker can play as a defender, but not as well as a defender; a violist can play the cello but not as well as a cellist. Let the team members choose the best role for themselves; one that fits their skills and talents and output will be maximized.

Typical problems and possible solutions

Dealing with team discontent

So what do you do with the trouble-makers? The cynics, the self-proclaimed experts, the naysayers? Simple. If you work in industry you fire them. I have fired people for not being team players even though their technical knowledge and expertise was in the upper quartile of the group. The loners and the rebels who refuse to work with the rest of the members make it extremely difficult to create, mould and maintain a successful team.

One of your children separates themselves from the rest of the family by devoting themselves to social media, interactive gaming and taking numerous selfies on their iPads – alone under the blue light. Troublemaker would be a bit harsh in this instance, maybe an independent separatist would be more appropriate – but disruptive to the family unit certainly. What do you do as the everyday leader?

Before seizing the laptop, or, at work, firing the person you have classified as 'trouble', take a look at yourself. Is there something about you, your attitudes, behaviours, habits that could have initiated the separation? Unlikely I agree, but always look in the mirror first when you encounter issues with those close to you. If, as I think you may reluctantly admit, you are close to perfect, then join your offspring in their world. Fully commit, spend the same hours as they do and try to discover the key to their happiness. Before asking them to make any changes, they have to accept you as an equal in their world. Then they might listen. Alternatively, they may be so motivated and inspired by the technology that they want to make a career out of it. Then why would you resist?

Turf wars

Turf wars are deadly. This is quite literally the case for criminal gangs in major cities, but also for organizations. They occur when either there is an overlap of defined responsibilities (easy to fix) or when one team attempts to take over some of the responsibilities of a sister team (less easy). It is less easy because one team believes, whether it's true or not, that the other team is not doing their job properly, and they start to do those jobs themselves. So it's time for the team leaders to suggest: 'Let's get together and sort this out.'

Situations when 'leading by letting go' can work

So where will 'leading by letting go' work? Let me tell you about an executive and his particular circumstances that I have attempted to help with a little informal coaching.

Let's call this leader James. James was recruited to lead a team of 150 people, replacing a manager who was retiring. He spoke at length with the retiring manager about the role and his team members. The retiring manager stated that his eight direct reports (DRs) were not very good and as a result he had another 24 people reporting directly to him – an unwieldy and unsustainable total of 32.

James and I discuss the situation and his plans. I said that if James outlines his plan for the future, his DRs will have had little or no input. It will be James' plan and not the team's plan. And as a result they may not buy in completely to his plan, but say nothing. After all, this is the new boss. Whilst this is the way that most handovers/takeovers go, I suggest to James that there is an alternative that he may want to consider.

At his first management team meeting James could ask for their input and set them an exercise:

'Ladies and Gentlemen – I have met you all individually and told you a little about me and my experience. While I have my own preferred leadership style and way of working, I don't want to impose a new system without understanding the good points and the bad points of the past. Please may I ask you to split into two teams, grab a flipchart each, and then record the good things from the previous regime and those that could be improved. When you're ready, bring the two teams together to compare notes and agree a prioritized list that you can talk me through. But I understand that you will need the freedom to express yourselves and discuss this privately and confidentially without me present – so I will leave you to it and I'll be back in an hour or so. Any questions?'

James would then leave the room, grab a coffee and think about the next exercise – how to handle his other 24 DRs. When he returns he would listen to his team headlining 'the good, the bad and the ugly', and thank them for their efforts. If the team had recommended fixes it was well and good, but if not, then he should set them another exercise. When James has exhausted the team's input, he will need to reflect on it. *'Brilliant, thanks a lot. Let me think about what you have told me and I'll come back to you in 48 hours with my decisions. But right now, I'd appreciate your advice about our future structure, as I only want a maximum of 12 DRs. So what options can you give me in how to re-structure the team which recognizes the other 24? Again I will leave you to discuss this privately and in confidence. I'll be in the cafeteria when you're through. Would another hour be enough for you to create three options for us all to move forward?'*

Notice the 'our' and 'us' above. Yes – it's James' team, but he's new – so for now at least, it would be better to demonstrate an intention to work collaboratively. James would defer on another caffeine fix and instead takes a walk.

By following the alternative plan above, I suggested to James that he would benefit in a number of ways; it would no longer be 'James' Plan' for the future, but rather the 'Team's Plan'; responsibility for execution will be shared; commitment will be higher; unknown pitfalls are more likely to be avoided; and any potential personality clashes within the group of 32 would be more likely to be reduced.

James decided to try my ideas and later sent this email: 'The workshop design has been very successful. No PowerPoints, a lot of post-its and sticky tape accumulating in a newly formed strategy. Many thanks for your suggestions and hints that has made me even more aware of the need for such an interactive approach. It prevented me from pushing my ideas onto the team too much.'

Leading by letting go is far more common today than it was even a decade ago, and the reason is simple. With the pace of technological change and the need for creative solutions to daily problems, we need more input from front-line employees. There is also the role of the so-called knowledge workers (KWs) that has become critical in some disciplines, organizations even, and fitting them into traditional command structures and reporting lines can stifle creative juices, restricting innovation. KWs insist on a high level of autonomy and independence in exchange for their passionate dedication to a highly specialized environment. And when successful they expect recognition and reward outside of the team norm. If the everyday manager does not 'let them go', they will go anyway, and seek an alternative more 'in-tune' employer. Managers should regard and treat their knowledge workers as if they were self-employed.

Final thoughts

So how good are you at 'letting go'? Try giving everyone more rope than you genuinely believe they can handle. Some will disappoint, but those that rise to the challenge will reward you handsomely.

How good are you at 'demanding and encouraging'? Demanding something from those who need encouragement will often demotivate them; but encouraging those that need a good kick will often prove ineffective. Switch. Alternate.

And for every team that recruits a new member; a new baby for the family; a new percussionist for the orchestra; a new striker for the football team; a new finance manager for an organization, adjustments to existing team roles will be required. You can't carry on as before. The new joiner will have talents and qualities that need to be integrated with their colleagues. It's your job to lead the adjustment.

Question. What changes would you ideally want to see in your loved ones, your local communities and your workplace? Draw up a list and then work to make them happen.

Changes in my loved ones	**Changes in my communities**	**Changes at work**

The Everyday Leader identifies those golden threads that weave through everyone in the team, and leverages these vital connections to build spirit and enthusiasm for a common goal that does good.
The Everyday Leader doesn't try to impose their ideas and ways of working on the team when alternatives may offer more benefit.
The Everyday Leader identifies a purpose that all team members can rally behind.

4

Leading with fairness

This chapter focuses on the need we all have to be treated fairly and the pressure that puts on the everyday leader. It also offers ways for leaders to test how fairly people believe they are being treated.

What is fairness and why it matters

Fairness in leadership is usually defined as making decisions free from favouritism and prejudice. But fair decision making also has a horizontal and vertical dimension. Horizontal fairness implies that we give people in the same situation the same treatment. It is sometimes referred to as the 'equal treatment of equals'. For example, if two people earn the same income (e.g. £15,000) they should both pay the same amount of income tax (e.g. £2,500). Horizontal fairness is why governments pass laws that ban discrimination on grounds such as race and gender. Vertical equity is defined as the unequal treatment of people in differing circumstances. In our income tax example, it would explain why it is considered fair for people with higher incomes to pay more proportionally in tax. The reason is that they have a higher ability to pay than someone with less income and hence a lower ability to pay.

These are not just theoretical issues; a lack of understanding of how people react to decisions that they deem to be unfair is one reason leaders often fail. Take the case of Margaret Thatcher, former Prime Minister of Britain. Her tenure as leader of the Conservative party and head of government was essentially brought down by a failure to consider the importance of vertical fairness.

In 1990, in an effort to rein in spending by local councils, Mrs Thatcher introduced what was known at the time as the poll tax. The poll tax was an example of a tax that met the horizontal fairness test (everyone paid a lump sum of £500 a year). Mrs Thatcher's logic was that since everyone had the same access to local council services, everyone should pay the same amount in tax. Unfortunately, a majority of the British population didn't see it that way. For those earning low incomes, the poll tax was a high proportion of their disposable income. Conversely, for those earning high incomes and with a greater ability to pay, £500 was a low percentage of earnings. The poll tax clearly violated the vertical fairness test and the riots and disruption caused by this unpopular decision caused Thatcher to resign.[1]

Examples of fairness inside and outside of work

So do you believe that you are a fair person? Is there a difference between fairness at work, in the world of sport or at home? Let's share some examples.

At home we hear the fairness cries: 'It's not fair that I have to do all the cooking.' 'It's not fair that you spend ten times more on clothes [or make-up] than I do.' 'It's not fair that you spend X and I can't spend Y.' 'It's not fair that I have to do the washing-up all the time.'

At work we are always dealing with fairness tests: 'It's not fair that Javid gets all the attention from upper management.' 'It's not fair that Seamus got promoted in front of me.' 'It's not fair that I have to stay in the country, while Wilhelm goes to Paris for the conference.' 'It's not fair that I have to do more for the same money as Ming who does less.'

We all know that life isn't fair. That's the reality, and learning to accept the fact is important for your health. Otherwise you will build bitterness and resentment, which will eat away at your equilibrium and tranquillity. But it still rankles, doesn't it? So where does our need for fairness originate? In childhood, our parents told us 'Don't be mean, Tommy, share your toys with Shanaya. Why don't you have five minutes with the sparkle wand, and then pass it to Shanaya so she can have five minutes with it. That's only fair.' We've all heard it, and said it. And it seems right.

As a grown up, you are driving and stuck in traffic, crawling forward nose-to-tail, when you notice in your door mirror that a vehicle is overtaking the whole line. They pass you, and then further up the road, they pull in to your line. It annoys you, and doesn't seem fair. Similarly, it's not fair that you paid a lot of money for your train ticket and can't get a seat.

The relative nature of fairness

Unfairness exists, and so does inequality. But is inequality the same as unfairness? Whether you answer yes or no, your answer is valid.

Because fairness is such a hugely relative concern, it is often in the eye of the beholder. No one can access a universally agreed-upon inequality continuum and check a 'fairness count' with which to challenge others. What you deem to be fair may not feel the same as it would to another person. And what you deem to be unfair, others could be unequivocal in their proclamation of fairness. And of course, some individuals are more sensitive to any unfairness or inequality whatever the circumstance; some more tolerant; while some see themselves as entitled to whatever they get, whether it's fair or not.

And yet, whatever you may think about fairness (such as, fair or not fair that some have so much more than others), what is less in doubt, is that the relative aspect of fairness has serious implications for how happy we feel. In Robert H. Frank's 1999 book *Luxury Fever: Why Money Fails to Satisfy in an Era of Excess*, the Cornell University economist makes the case that we are hardwired (for various biological and psychological reasons) to measure our personal standing in relation to what others have. In other words, we assess fairness and try to achieve happiness not by improving our absolute standing, but by improving our standing relative to others. In Frank's words, 'evidence from the large scientific literature on the determinants of subjective well-being consistently suggests that we have strong concerns about relative position.' For example, if your neighbour didn't buy his new Mercedes Benz, you probably wouldn't have felt the need for the latest-and-greatest Jaguar, and you and your neighbour would have certainly worked less, and spent more time with your loved ones and invested in meaningful experiences that bring you joy.

Frank's thesis on runaway consumption and the extravagant luxury spending that puts people into debt, has important implications for our understanding of what is seen as 'fair' in an income sense and seems as valid now as it was when his book was published in 1999 at the height of the dot-com boom.[2]

Fairness in pay and monetary rewards

The UK's High Pay Centre's (HPC's) examination of the pay of chief executives of FTSE100 companies, published in August 2016, showed a rise in the gap between the average employee's pay package and the CEO's. In 2015 the biggest pay packet in each company was on average 129 times bigger than the average employee's. But less than 20 years ago, it was a mere 47 times and 50 years ago it was a multiple in the single digits.

But don't expect too much to change if Sainsbury's chief executive, Mike Coupe, is any indication. After announcing the proposed merger with Asda (a Walmart subsidiary), in 2018, Coupe, 57, was caught singing the song, 'we're in the money', as he prepared for a television interview about the merger. Coupe's pay was to go up from £2.4 million per annum to £3.4 million, a 42 per cent increase. At the other end of the pay spectrum, 9,000 of his staff would be losing the equivalent of about £400 per annum as the Company strips away some of their benefits. What appalling leadership and quite an obvious contravention of the Golden Rule – he should not be asking his staff to lose any amount, unless he himself leads by example and loses the same or more.

Siobhain McDonagh, the Labour MP representing Mitcham & Morden, castigated Coupe for forcing 'his dedicated staff to work well, for less'. (This was a reference to Sainsbury's advertising strapline, 'live well for less'.) She asked Mr Coupe: 'What self-respecting chief executive would accept a million-pound pay rise while simultaneously slashing the salaries of 9,000 of his most loyal and long-standing staff?'[3] Perhaps the cries of unfairness were ultimately heard in the halls of government, as the proposed merger would eventually be disallowed by the authorities.

Triggers of unfairness at work

We all know that the distribution of money isn't fair. Early in his career, my son was angry when notified of his annual bonus. To me it was a significant sum, and at a level that I had never earned. 'I'm not happy with the amount. It's not fair that Jack got a lot more and did less for it!' My son was not at all unhappy with the actual figure, but rather its relationship with what he perceived his colleague received. This example is a confirmation of what Robert Frank observed happening in the US and other countries in the late 1990s and is a genuine fairness challenge for all everyday leaders, like you. How would you convince my son that his bonus was fair? We'll come to that later.

In a 2013 survey, the Chartered Institute of Personnel and Development (CIPD) asked a number of questions about fairness of a nationally representative sample of 2,067 employees in the CIPD Employee Outlook survey.[4] It found that:

- rules and agreed procedures are not applied consistently by decision makers;
- rewards are not distributed fairly;

- resources are not distributed fairly;
- the basis for policies designed to make decisions 'fairer' are not clear to most of the employees affected; and
- there is a lack of consultation among those who will be affected by the implementation of decisions.

Triggers of unfairness that respondents quoted were, in order:

1. Pay (freeze, long hours, senior management pay/bonuses, differences in pay).
2. Workload (distribution).
3. Bullying/victimization/harassment.
4. Favouritism.
5. Forced redundancy/redundancy procedures.
6. Promotion decisions.
7. Flexible work (as it relates to task, time, and so on).
8. Performance review system/appraisal.
9. Pension decisions/schemes.
10. Changes to employment terms and conditions.
11. Age/gender/disability discrimination.
12. Unfair dismissal.
13. Respect.
14. Lack of voice.
15. Disciplinary procedures/actions.
16. Work hours.

17 Job downgrades with larger role size.

18 Reward system.

All the 18 points are cumulative pressures on a person. The level of pressure will of course vary between individuals. When the pressure rises and reaches a personal threshold level for one individual then one of two things normally happens: they seek alternative employment and resign, although many resign without the safety net of another job offer; or they mentally resign their commitment and loyalty to the organization and soldier on. Pensions consultancy Barnett Waddingham interviewed 3,000 UK workers in 2018 to understand health and wellbeing in the workplace.[5] The research showed that 36 per cent admitted to coasting at work, and, of them, 41 per cent didn't see themselves in the job in 12 months. They had mentally resigned. From the organization's perspective the literal resignation is best. I wonder how many of the second category are living or working in your family or organization right now, causing damage to the unit's performance and morale by doing the minimum.

Consultation with affected parties lessens feelings of unfairness

Let's assume now that you are on the receiving end of a fresh announcement at work: a new job grading scale, a new pay freeze being introduced; the announcement of a new downsizing scheme. How do you react? For example, let me place your gut reaction to hearing the news of a wage freeze on an imaginary fairness continuum here:

Fair	Unfair

'That's not fair!' An emotional, de Bono 'red hat' thinking result.[6] But did you understand the events, thought processes, and the options that were considered by the decision makers before scoring? No. Because if you had done, then it wouldn't have been a gut reaction. So would you agree that if you had been privy to all that information then perhaps your rating would have been different?

This means that before big stuff is contemplated, it is essential for everyday leaders, the adults in the family; the team leader; and the senior executive, to communicate:

- the background;
- the process objective;
- the factors involved;
- the consultation process;
- the names of those invited to comment;
- any weighting that is to be applied, and if so to which factors

before any decision is reached. Then to check, via town hall meetings, a survey etc., whether those affected believe it is fair. For the family it can be as simple as 'Is that OK with everyone?' and for the team or organization you may want to consider – depending on the size – a professionally designed employee survey.

Armed with knowledge about the background and process, then even if you disagree with the outcome, maybe you won't think it's as arbitrary and unfair as you initially believed. This is what researchers like to call 'procedural justice' and the evidence is clear: fairness in process matters as much, and sometimes more, than the actual outcome.[7]

Asking, 'Is everyone OK with that…? [Pause] Good,' may be OK at home, but it is certainly not OK in the community or at work. Because silence may be the only weapon team members have to voice an opinion. Silence is not a sign of approval but one of underlying unease. Instead, what about offering to leave the room and say, 'I have been told to take silence as a negative response, so, without me present, work together to produce a list of objections to what I proposed, and I'll listen.'

But: 'John, I simply haven't got the time for all that. In my organization, that would take weeks and we don't have weeks. I will have to make a decision.' I know. It's not fair that you have to go through all that. But, if you don't, then think about the possible degradation of morale, the feelings of unfairness about your decision, and the potential for some employees to mentally resign their commitment and loyalty. It's not fair either way. But at least if you make the effort to listen and explain, the upset felt by affected parties can be mitigated.

What you can do to create fair policies and make sure that they're adopted

As pay was listed as the number one reason for unfairness in the CIPD survey list of triggers, why not consider inviting a front-line-paid employee onto the senior Remuneration Committee? Give them an equal voice and equal vote as their colleagues. They could be an excellent communication representative offering a 'voice' to different levels of the organization. (As an aside, I remember Malcolm Fallen, the then-CEO of Kingston Communications plc., telling me that he often accompanied one of their engineers for a day working in the field, so that he could understand, first-hand, the working conditions, general workforce morale and any 'hot issues'. Standard stuff, but then he surprised me when he said, 'And then I ask that same person to accompany me for a day doing my job.' Brilliant!)

Reuters reported that outsourcing group, Capita, announced in mid-2018 that it would appoint two employees to its board of directors, so that the voice of its 77,000 staff would be heard directly. Their CEO, Jonathan Lewis said, 'Our people are fundamental to our success and it seems inappropriate to me to not be represented on the board.' The pair will enjoy the same rights and privileges as the other non-executive directors.

In Germany, this idea of allowing for worker voice at the top of the corporate decision making pyramid is known as the principle of 'co-determination'. In all major companies with supervisory boards of directors, worker representatives are entitled to make up half of the board. It's a great way for upper management – whether they like it or not – to hear from workers before policies get implemented into action. And it allows workers to better understand why management needs to take the actions that it does. As a result, although Germany is not immune to work disruptions, it has historically had one of the lowest strike rates in the Western world, much lower than Britain or even the United States, despite the latter countries having much lower union representation.

OK, so let's assume that you have developed and communicated, for example, best-in-class Equality, Fairness and Ethics policies for your organization as an everyday leader. 'In this family, we don't tell lies'; 'In this team we respect the differences of opinion of our colleagues'; 'In this organization we encourage whistleblowing'. Great but how do you know that people act and work in accordance with the policies? These structures might help:

- family meetings;
- regular opinion surveys at least annually, and additionally when issue specific;
- helplines – with an anonymous option;
- workers councils;
- trade unions.

Again, involving and allowing these structures to form inside your unit allows for less unilateral decision making, which you might argue reduces efficiency. But how efficient was it for Margaret Thatcher to have found out many months later that her Poll Tax was not going to be accepted by the British Public? Would it not have been fairer and more efficient for her government to have consulted prior to making that change and realized that this scheme could backfire? Could they not have taken that opportunity to explain their logic to the public and perhaps lessened the discontent?

In business, research shows that companies that involve their employees in decision making and that provide employee representation structures like joint consultative committees (as found in Germany under their works council system) outperform those companies that prefer instead to run their companies on a command and control style. It's cliché now to use this term, but it's no less true: you *can* as a leader *do well, by doing good*. And as a leader, you should feel confident to push through with reforms that make decision-making more open and transparent and that involve more participants, even if other managers and those with power feel uncomfortable. The costs of slowing down a decision is made up for by the perceived fairness of the process and by the quality of the eventual outcome.

Final thoughts

In life, as at work, we witness inequality and unfairness everywhere. At school; applying for a job; getting a home; at work; in retirement; even in death. The everyday leader knows this but doesn't try to change the world. Instead she tries to change *her* world and the perceptions of those around her. The Buddha teaches that when our desires, our craving, our constant discontent with what we have, and our continual longing for more and more causes us suffering, then we should stop doing it.[8] Make a difference between what we need, and what we want. Strive for our needs, modify our wants. Needs can be met, but wants are never-ending. Will getting and acquiring more make you happy? Searching the internet for lottery winners that wished they had never won will throw up many examples. If I asked you to compile a list of things that you and your family want, how many items would be on there? Let's suppose that I wave a magic wand and you get everything you want. I bet you'll soon start another list of wants. Needs should be the focus and prioritized over desires and cravings.

Question. Think of one or two areas which you believe are unfair. Then create a few ways by which you can attract followers to your way of thinking, and thereby start a movement for change.

Examples	**Ways to attract agreement**
Unfair example	
Unfair example	

The Everyday Leader doesn't decide what is fair without first socializing and collecting reaction to a proposal from as broad an array of people as possible
The Everyday Leader lets the voice of those affected by a decision to be heard in a transparent way, so as to ensure the process is seen as 'just'.
The Everyday Leader realizes that 'fairness' is a relative concept, that to some is settled by treating people in similar circumstances the same, while for others it involves locating sources of difference and treating people accordingly.

5

Leading from behind

As a leader, your followers expect you to tell them what to do. But this chapter explains that leadership can often be most effective when the use of authority is hidden deliberately from plain sight, where a command and control culture would be unhelpful at best and counter-productive at worst. Leading from behind, or by standing behind the scenes, essentially means the subtle empowerment of others to carry out an objective set from above, just as the shepherd lets their sheep graze but uses their dog to steer and corral the sheep. But it's not easy and success will depend on the ability of everyday leaders to subordinate their natural instincts and traditional behaviour.

A common example of leading from the front: John, a young boy of 7, likes to play ball games in the garden. Parent to child: 'John, it's time for you to cut the grass and clean-up the dog mess.' John replies, 'Oh, do I have to?'

Contrast that example with the following approach: John likes to play ball games in the garden. Parent lets the grass grow and the dog to foul the lawn. John will find it increasingly difficult and unpleasant to continue his football and tennis knock-about. So, John finally says

'Mum, the garden is such a mess and Dad hasn't told me to do anything about it for ages.' 'Never mind son, why don't you play on the computer instead?' 'Nah, I've just finished another Fortnite session and it's nice weather outside. I think I'll do a bit of a clear-up myself.' 'Congratulations, Son!' Mum avoids a 'thank you' as it implies that what John is doing is for his mum and not himself. Using a word like 'congratulations' serves to foster self-motivation and makes it about them and not you.

This idea is not new by the way. It was recognized by none other than Jean-Jacques Rousseau, the 18th century Geneva-born French 'philosophe' in his famous book, *Émile, or On Education*. Émile refers to the name of a fictional boy that is taught by Rousseau in the role of teacher. The book is a treatise on the role of education, which Rousseau considered to be the 'best and most important' of all his writings. Rousseau argued for more freedom, insisting that children needed to learn for themselves and be given the room and space to do so. But crucially, Rousseau was not relinquishing the leadership roles to be played by parents and teachers.[1]

Contending that the traditional means of teaching moral character through discipline and learning by rote produced tyrants and slaves, Rousseau proposed to teach Émile by exposing him to situations and learning environments that would generate life experiences from which to learn from. By barking out orders and setting about tasks (leading from the front), the parent/teacher paradoxically loses control. This is because, in order to get your child to do what you want them to do, you are forced into giving rewards and negotiating trade-offs. This approach was famously encapsulated by Rousseau, when he stated:

> When education is most carefully attended to, the teacher issues his orders and thinks himself master, but it is the child who is really master. He uses the tasks you set him to obtain what he wants from you, and he can always make you pay for an hour's industry by a week's complaisance. You must always be making bargains with him. These bargains, suggested in your fashion, but carried out in his, always follow the direction of his own fancies, especially when you are foolish enough to make the condition some advantage he is almost sure to obtain, whether he fulfils his part of the bargain or not.

Rousseau's teacher offered the boy choice but controlled him through the choices made available. In the following paragraph Rousseau points out the power involved in leading from behind the scenes:

> Take the opposite course with your pupil; let him always think he is master while you are really master. There is no subjection so complete as that which preserves the forms of freedom; it is thus that the will itself is taken captive.[2]

As Rousseau well understood, leading from behind is a key component of developing self-motivation, which we will discuss further in Chapter 12. Of course, with the grass growing above head height and the dog refusing to make additional deposits until more space is created, you may have to try an alternative tactic and become quite direct. But is waiting and allowing someone to come to a realization before imploring them into action worth a shot? Absolutely!

The strategy behind 'leading from behind'

Leading from behind *is* a strategy. It's deliberate and considered. It's not about giving way and letting another person make the decisions. It is about giving way and letting someone else make the decisions, *but* within a framework that you have constructed, and within which, you remain in overall control. Like a toddler on one of those extendable leads, they are free to wander, but if they try to go too far, they reach the end of the line.

Do you like being told what to do? Some people do, some don't like responsibility and want others to make all of the decisions; some don't like to think. But others prefer to have some input into the planned actions. 'Darling, would you re-decorate the sitting-room please?' versus 'Darling, would you please re-paint the sitting-room walls? Make sure you protect the carpet and furniture properly, stir the paint vigorously before you begin, and then start with the window wall. Use the small angled brush to cut-in at the wall/ceiling joint, then the two inch brush so that you can then have the space to use the roller freely. And remove your best watch otherwise it will get spotted.' Which request allows for more discretion? Which one will produce a better result?

Generally speaking, people don't mind being asked to do something, but often resent being told *how* to do it. And with knowledge workers you can't tell them how to do it anyway, because you don't know.

A 'what if' scenario: you have been made head coach of Chelsea football club

Let's assume that Roman Abramovich, owner of Premiere League's Chelsea Football Club, appoints you as the new Chelsea manager. You know absolutely nothing about football, but for some reason Roman wanted you, as you had previously come to his notice when you were instrumental in helping him secure a big business deal. Your next match is on Saturday against the mighty Arsenal. You gather together the first team squad at 9am and tell them that another meeting will be held at 4pm, at which time you expect <u>them</u> to tell you:

- Arsenal's likely team selection;
- the opponent's probable tactics;
- their strengths and weaknesses (physical and mental);
- the lessons we learned the last time we played Arsenal;
- our preferred team selection and tactics;
- the name of the player who will, during play, adjust team tactics to stifle specific threats;
- the changes they would like to see to pre-match-day preparation and routine.

You hand them a copy of these tasks and give them some encouragement: 'You are all fantastic athletes with amazing skills. I'm told you work very well together and have a winning mentality. I can't wait to hear what you have decided as a game plan. Good luck.'

Twenty-two multi-millionaires gather together in shock, some laughing nervously; some feeling insulted by your appointment; some refusing to cooperate entirely; some calling their agent to get a transfer. But once they have drawn breath, talked openly to each other about their feelings and argued about the task, eventually someone will look at your questions and recall your five-minute briefing, before saying, 'OK, so what are we going to do guys? Who's going to do what?'

At 4pm they present their responses and answers to your questions. It doesn't matter what their plan is, how good or how bad. It doesn't matter that you don't understand it. It's their plan. At the end you nod, smile broadly and say, 'Gentlemen, congratulations on a brilliant response, and thank you for your efforts. A great plan and I love it! Through this exercise I have learned a lot about the game and a lot more about you as professionals. So, go out and execute your plan. I can't wait to see how well you do it. Good luck!'

Admitting what you don't know and asking the right questions

Notice the use of words like 'your plan' and 'you do it' in the scenario above. Do not be troubled by a lack of knowledge or certainty. No-one has all the answers, and some don't have any answers. However, it *is* important that you know what you don't know, and by that I mean, that you admit to yourself and others that your knowledge and understanding of certain topics is limited, e.g. the football offside rule, or how to read a balance sheet.

But everyday leaders have confidence in their own ability to ask the right questions. Good questions generate answers that can get to the heart of an issue. But you'll need to adopt a detective's attitude and methodology, keeping the questions flowing until you feel satisfied that you have uncovered the underlying truth. This is a fundamental skill for leading from behind, as a 'good question' makes the subject stop, and take a moment to consider their response. And it is this stopping and thinking that is your goal. With a bit of luck, they will continue thinking about your interrogation after you've gone, and then start to think, as we all do, of alternative answers that would have been far better.

- 'Why are you not taking more care with your personal hygiene?' (For your teenagers, not work colleagues.)
- 'Why do you record that data and who uses it?'
- 'What do you think is the main reason the plan might fail?' (Known as 'pre-mortem' thinking.)
- 'What have been the lessons learned from previous projects like this one?'
- 'How will you measure success?'
- 'How will you get back from the disco?'
- 'Where would we go to get this done?'
- 'Where would I look to find how others have approached a similar problem?'
- 'When would you step in to stop further confusion?'
- 'What are you packing before you go to Amir's, and how will you get there?'
- 'Who makes the final decision, using what criteria?'
- 'Who else was part of the discussion and what did they have to say?'

Remember it's not about <u>me</u> . . . it's about <u>you</u>

Personally, I find post-match television interviews with football managers always reveal more than a little of their individual ability to lead from behind. Did they say, 'We were brilliant today' or did they say, 'They were brilliant today'. Was it: 'They were poor today', 'We were poor today', or 'Our performance was poor today?' Do they refer to the squad as 'My team'? And if so, why? The players belong to the club, not the manager. He doesn't own the players. When the coach gets fired the players remain. It is 'the team' not 'my team'.

On this same point, political leaders often think they own the party they lead 'My party is determined... etc.' No, it should be 'the party' or 'our party'. 'My party' subordinates thousands of members to a secondary role, and it demeans them. So it's not 'my company' or 'my team', it's the 'workers, customers, shareholders' company and it's the 'players, fans, supporters' team.

One of the greatest leaders in recent times, Nelson Mandela said:

> It is better to lead from behind and to put others in front, especially when you celebrate victory when nice things occur. You take the front line when there is danger. Then people will appreciate your leadership.

And in his 1994 autobiography, *Long Walk to Freedom*, Mandela also described it this way:

> I always remember the regent's axiom: a leader, he said, is like a shepherd. He stays behind the flock, letting the most nimble go out

ahead, whereupon the others follow, not realizing that all along they are being directed from behind.

But if you have a strong personality, are an *alpha* type, or love micromanaging, you will be challenged on your:

- ability to communicate in different ways; to tell without telling, to speak without talking;
- ability to 'hold back' and restrain your natural instincts to take-over;
- ability to resist dropping in to the mix a little bit of your undoubted wisdom;
- ability not to show-off;
- comfort, pride even, in letting others take the limelight, without your name being mentioned;
- comfort level with mistakes being made and your ability subsequently to hold-off from apportioning blame.

And when anyone comes to you and asks for advice, resist giving it. Put your 'coaching head' on and instead ask them for some ideas of how to move forward. 'I have a problem boss and I feel stuck, what should I do?' Your first response should be, 'What are your options?'

Even if you're not an alpha, the challenges posed are significantly more profound than at first you may think. It is not unusual for a manager to feel a genuine sense of loss that the obvious power they enjoyed has evaporated; they may feel unneeded, redundant, disenfranchised, unloved; their role and identity questioned.

Emasculated. Consequences can be serious if these feelings are not acknowledged beforehand and discussed openly.

Letting go, and getting more back in return

In politics the use of behind the scenes leadership is quite common. The overthrow of Libyan strongman Colonel Gaddafi in 2011 was preceded by protests, and then by a full-scale rebellion against the dictator. Western countries became increasingly concerned. Calls for action became louder and eventually irresistible. But as Western armed forces were, and remain still, unwelcome on the sands of North Africa and the Middle East, the United States searched first for partners and then for an internationally acceptable disguise for their intent. It came in the form of the Arab League, who were persuaded to propose to the UN Security Council, a 'no-fly' zone in Libya to prevent the regime's indiscriminate bombing of civilians. The US then used the Arab League's position to win UN support for a far larger military intervention. Unfortunately, no one planned for the aftermath of deposing a despot who had been in power for nearly 50 years, and there is still violence and tumult in Libya.

Many of you will be familiar with *The Prince*, possibly the first ever attempt to provide a guide for sustained political success. The work by Niccolò Machiavelli, published in 1513, provoked outrage at the time, and in the years following, the adjective *Machiavellian* has become a pejorative term for describing cunning deception and intrigue, usually at the highest levels of governments and organizations. And quite possibly – your family. For example, your children can be 'innocently' *Machiavellian* all the time:

> 'Mum, can I have an ice cream?'
> 'Not now sweetheart.'
> 'Mum, why can't I have an ice cream?'
> 'It'll spoil your dinner, so better to wait until afterwards, eh'
> 'Mum, if I promise to eat all of my dinner, can I have an ice cream?'
> 'That's a no, sweetheart. Now go and play outside for a while.'

Pause, as the wisdoms of Niccolò are automatically and subconsciously evaluated for effect and the likelihood of success, your child finds Dad alone in the backyard reading the paper:

> 'Dad, I fancy an ice cream. Do you want a chocolate one or a strawberry one?'
> 'All right, Son, enjoy. Chocolate for me but with nuts on, please!'

Deception and manipulation for personal gain. Niccolò would be proud.

I mention this example here, not to recommend any of the concepts that Machiavelli espouses, but rather to forewarn you about becoming an innocent victim of the political manoeuvrings of others. You can be led from behind without even knowing it, particularly in large organizations.

I remember one of my bosses from yesteryear who was permanently suspicious of everyone and everything. He was always 'on-guard' for Machiavellians. Greeting him with a jovial 'Good morning!', he would stop and search my demeanour and body language for clues as to my hidden intentions; what did I *really* want; was he being led somewhere inadvertently? He was acutely aware of Machiavellians' ability to lead from behind with amoral and unethical intent.

In the meantime don't become too paranoid about your child's intentions. Sometimes, you just have to enjoy the ice cream.

Leading from behind, but with genuine empowerment

When Ricardo Semler entertains us with his TED lectures, he uses a number of thought-provoking soundbites, such as: 'We have got comfortable working on a Sunday evening, checking emails etc., and yet we remain uncomfortable going to the cinema on a Monday afternoon.' He says we have to learn to sit with our ice cream, popcorn and drink, free from all guilt when our colleagues are working. I'm sure you are familiar with Semler's transformational leadership style, described so brilliantly in his book, *Maverick*, but if you're not, then may I recommend it to you? In the meantime here's a quick *precis*.

In 1980, when Semler was just 21 years old, he took over as CEO of the family business from his father. Upon taking control, he fired 60 per cent of the top managers, empowered front-line staff to make their own decisions and tore up the company rulebook.

Over the following years, Semler has been a consistent leader from behind, allowing employees to set their own working hours, pay, holiday etc., whilst encouraging ideas and entrepreneurial behaviours. It has paid-off handsomely, but some of the original staff were uncomfortable with the new freedoms and have been replaced, through a process of natural attrition or what economists like to call 'self-selection'. These are fancy ways of saying that those that didn't like taking on more responsibility left, and were replaced over time by those who did.

Now, though most people do want more say in their everyday lives, not everyone does. Leading from behind will not work with those whose have little or no interest in getting more involved with the aims and objectives of the team, be it in a family or in an organization. They may not want to participate in the decision-making, their temperament and attitude being more isolationist. In those cases you have to decide whether to abandon attempts to lead from behind, which would have given you more flexibility and time, or to resume or adopt a more autocratic style. If you decide to continue then you may have to replace those who find it difficult to work with more latitude. In the case of families or cultures where consensus decision-making prevails, the issue is more complex and requires a different set of approaches that we highlight below.

Everyone can do it, but not everyone wants to or can

If leading from behind means the subtle empowerment of others to carry out your bidding, then it follows that everyone can be a leader from behind. The skill, art even, seems to have been one of the first ones for which children have been hardwired. They have become especially adept as they practice every day. Imagine this scenario when the child, for whatever reason, decides that they don't want to go to school today, but know that it's Mum that makes the decision. Subterfuge needed as follows:

> 'Mummy, my tummy hurts.' [Delivered in a shallow whiny voice, accompanied by hand gesture to stomach.]
>
> Mum feels said tum, then forehead for temperature, pushing back hair before declaring her expert medical opinion:
>
> 'Probably something you ate, it'll soon pass. Go and get your school things ready.'
>
> 'Aarghhh . . .'

If you're a parent or recall a similar childhood instance, no doubt you know the rest.

But if you're not a parent or don't recall your four-year-old self, let me play it out for you: the child ends up staying at home and you end up ringing your employer telling them your child is ill and you have no babysitter option, thus you'll be working from home for the day! Child leading parent from behind.

So the art of subtle empowerment is not only for those at the top of the tree. Anyone can do it. But people in some cultures find it easier to lead than in others. In some cultures there is more deference paid to authority figures and those more senior who are deemed to be wiser. Take the case of *Korean Air Cargo* flight 8509, which crashed after take-off at London Stansted airport on 22 December 1999. The plane crashed because the first officer and flight engineer did not stop the captain from continuing to roll the aircraft to port until the left wing hit the ground.[3] Tragically, all four on board were killed. The investigation showed that the captain's instruments gave him misleading information, whilst the first officer's readings were accurate. Large aircraft don't normally bank more than 30 degrees from the horizontal and yet the relatively inexperienced first officer watched as the roll continued past 30 degrees. He knew this was highly unusual, but he never questioned the captain's actions. Leading from behind, he might have chosen words like:

'My instruments are showing different readings to yours, Captain.'

'I've never seen you bank more than 30 degrees before, Captain.'

'This doesn't feel right, Captain.'

Sometimes we defer some authority to others because we know far less (the Chelsea coaching example). My next door neighbours, husband and wife, are both software engineers. I have to confess that I don't really know what software engineers do every day. And I would find it difficult to set them a coherent objective. So, as a technically ignorant everyday leader, I would have no choice but to lead from behind.

But as a behind-the-scene leader, I wouldn't relinquish complete control. I might get help from those who organize so-called 'hackathons' or 'hackfests'. The goal of any hackathon is to create a usable application. As you know, hackathons usually start with a few presentations to teams of computer geeks and enthusiasts about the challenge they have been set, the context of their challenge, the time limits, if any, and the prizes on offer. Hackathons run uninterrupted until the teams present and demonstrate their trial solutions. The teams work through the night[s], surviving on power naps, pizza and energy drinks – intensive effort to produce an app.

To give you an example: in 2014, the British Government helped to set up the world's first hackathon dedicated to improving the lives of people living with dementia. The workshops have been staged every year since, and in 2017, one of the winning teams developed Memo, a personal assistant that passively collects the frequency of repeated questions (a symptom of dementia), such as: 'What day is it today?' Memo then analyses the data and produces a report for clinicians to evaluate. Brilliant!

The increasing role of technology in leading all of us from behind

Social media can prove to be a powerful weapon in shaping the responses by governments, organizations large and small, and by your family. The revelations of Facebook being used by Russian trolls to influence voters in both the 2016 Brexit vote and the US Presidential election are two of the most obvious examples. But it is not limited to those two instances. Utterances and the written word are examined and dissected microscopically for hidden prejudices by huge swathes of on-liners who delight in calling the perceived so-called transgression. Electors, workers and family members who felt powerless in the past have found their voice online. 'The government should increase spending on health-care.'; 'The Company should pay women the same as men doing the same job.' 'In a recent survey, we found that our pocket money is the lowest of everyone on this street, and probably the whole world!'

Advances in social technology have shifted the balance of power away from single 'fashion/influence leaders' in favour of 'mass online opinion'. Many senior decision makers, including the family heads, may see this as a threat to their ability to steer the bus on a route of their choosing; a restriction on the freedoms they enjoyed previously. However, I would argue that their ability to steer the bus to the terminus would be more effective if they accessed the social media road signs and checked the speed limits.

Final Thoughts

I love those television programmes that ask the boss to work incognito with the ground floor workers and get the low-down on what is really happening in their organization. For me, it is remarkable how often the boss lacks awareness of serious shortcomings. So my question is this – are the shortcomings of your team, family or organisation being camouflaged by an overly command and control culture?

Question. Think of some tactics/tools that can lead a person or group from behind at home, with friends, and at work:

Name at home	**Name or names of friends**	**Name or group at work**
Possible tactics		

The Everyday Leader encourages the leadership skills of others and gives them more rope and scope than they initially think is appropriate... but not so much that they fall down the well unable to climb back up.
The Everyday Leader doesn't demotivate others by adding 'but' at the end of a 'pat-on-the-back' such as, 'I think that's a great idea, but . . .'
The Everyday Leader stands behind his followers.
The Everyday Leader always knows the 'end goal' or 'direction' that the empowered team is heading towards.

6

Leading large groups

This chapter demonstrates how to reach out to a much wider audience, initiating or reinforcing the link you have with them.

If you have decided, as an everyday leader, to try to influence or persuade a wide audience, then as we shall see in the next chapter, you may consider using the media, and its voracious appetite for news and stories, to your advantage. Writing letters to editors can also prove a very effective way to lead from behind, as they may pick-up the theme of what you write and develop it themselves.

For me, the greatest demonstration of inspiring a large group and a much wider community in recent decades, was a very simple event watched by millions. Nelson Mandela decided to wear the same Number 6 jersey as Captain Francois Pienaar at the opening of the Rugby World Cup final at Ellis Park in Johannesburg in 1995. On the pitch and wearing the jersey and team cap, he shook the captain's hand and wished him good luck. As Mandela turned, Francois noticed that it was his own number 6 jersey that Mandela was wearing and he said afterwards that he was overwhelmed with emotion and filled with immense pride.[1] The match was a thriller, South Africa winning 15–12 after extra time. That act, an iconic moment in sport, in front of the home crowd and millions around the world watching on television, closed the door on the previous apartheid system. No words were needed, yet the effects were hugely motivational on a number of disparate, even opposing groups.

Let's think of the groupings and communities that were affected by that gesture:

- The rugby team itself – players, coaches, support staff etc.
- The South African team supporters at the stadium and around the world.
- The emergent South African nation – a symbol of togetherness – black and white.
- International businesses – demonstrating to investors a nation at peace with itself – a stable platform for inward investment.

And it also set the example to other majority leaders in the country – this is the way Mandela wanted it to be – a genuine hand of friendship offered to previous oppressors. I wonder how many options were drafted and then considered to satisfy the above demands before the decision was made to simply wear the shirt and cap? Pure genius.

Tapping into the 'Mandela' in all of us

I'm no Mandela and neither are you, but what a fantastic example to all of us, of when a simple human emotional connection can out-power past hate and distrust, and be significantly more motivational than pages of 'management speak'. The everyday leader thinks about emotional connections often.

But if you have to use 'management speak' as part of your job, then follow Warren East's example. East took over as the Chief Executive of Rolls Royce plc in 2015. His job was to stabilize and then restore the Company to profitable growth. I interviewed him at Rolls Royce's Derby factory in 2016 and he was very open about the challenges he faced as leader. Like Nelson, he had and still has to communicate with many big groups and stakeholders; customers; suppliers, employees, company pensioners; government ministers; civil servants; journalists; shareholders, commentators, to name a few.

When East assumed the leadership, all the stakeholders were nervous because they had received a number of profit forecast downgrades from previous executives.

East's primary job is to construct and communicate an inspiring vision of the future when customers are happier, jobs are secure and shareholders are satisfied with their return. At that time the Rolls Royce vision was:

> *Rolls-Royce's vision is to be the market-leader in high performance power systems where our engineering expertise, global reach and deep industry knowledge deliver outstanding customer relationships and solutions. We operate across five businesses: Civil Aerospace, Defence Aerospace, Marine, Nuclear and Power Systems.*

Interestingly, the vision six months later under East's leadership was:

Better power for a changing world.

Better power – Helping our customers do more, using less

Better future – Committed to innovation, powering better, cleaner growth

Better business – Investing in technology, people and ideas to improve all aspects of our performance.

The vision was simpler and more focused. I love the 'better' in everything. It communicates a level of dissatisfaction with the current situation, a drive for improvement, and establishes momentum in moving forward.

But three years later, the Rolls Royce vision is even more sharply focused:

Rolls-Royce pioneers cutting edge technologies that deliver the cleanest, safest and most competitive solutions to meet our planet's vital power needs.

Telling the world that you are a pioneer will attract the most talented innovators and inventors even in fields traditionally thought outside of the engineering domain. The words 'pioneer' and 'cutting edge' state the Company's leadership role in the development of power systems, attracting new customer enquiries. And employees have more spring in their step as they are inspired and energized to investigate the radical. Brilliant.

The challenges of leading big groups: the example of building a house

Leading big groups and other stakeholders is often a daunting and thankless task for the everyday leader. You'll be frustrated by indifference, inefficiency and an almost insurmountable resistance to change. And you'll find that individuals make decisions, if they make any decisions at all, on the basis of how it will affect them personally.

Let's assume you work in a large organization, and decide to make a suggestion to improve something – be it quality, timeliness, cost or relevance. But before doing anything please read the previous paragraph again.

Let me choose a specific challenge, dissect it and offer some recommendations for you to consider. When you next hear yourself say that 'somebody should do something about that', decide that as one of the everyday leaders, that someone is you.

Now, instead of building a huge and powerful aircraft engine, I am choosing the building of a house as your goal. The objective for this imagined project is to ensure that in the future, all new houses are snag-free on moving-in day, and remain so for the first few months.

There is no regulatory uniformity for the building industry in Western countries, so I will select the United Kingdom and its regulatory framework as the example. But the principles I outline can, of course, apply to other countries and indeed to other non-building related projects.

Here is a simple project model with five stages:

Stage 1 – List the various stakeholders and their interests.

Stage 2 – Select target groups and individuals.

Stage 3 – Contact them with an appeal to their agenda not yours.

Stage 4 – List your demands.

Stage 5 – Negotiate changes and celebrate success.

At the outset you have to decide what success looks like. What is your objective? What are you trying to achieve? Write it down. Here's my goal: Success = More homes, fewer faults

Below is my personal judgement on who the various stakeholders are and what they want. This is based on anecdotal evidence collected from various parties during the snag corrections on my new home in 2017/8. I have not tried to contact these groupings directly to confirm the interests I quote. Instead I have used my own judgement as you will have to on your project. But do spend some time on the stakeholder listing, as often what you deem to be bit-part players, may hold the key to unlock the logjam of inaction and indifference.

Stage 1 – list the various stakeholders and their interests

UK government	Wants to see a significant rise in the number of new homes being built to address the housing shortage.
House builders	Want profit and a good reputation, but profit comes before reputation. Want new techniques in order to build homes faster. Want quicker and less costly planning procedures. Want faster decisions from local authorities.
Sub-contractors	Want instructions from head office and from site managers to be as early as possible. Two issues here: firstly, notice to get sub-contractors' tradespeople on site (four weeks); secondly, a work schedule from the site manager to the tradespeople supervisor for specific work on named properties (seven days). Want payment on time.

Tradespeople	Want all materials available at properties on site at least three days before they are required for fitting. Don't want to be called from one job to address an issue on another as it disrupts work.
Skills Shortage/ Apprentices	There is a national skill shortage. Many self-proclaimed tradespeople are unqualified, inexperienced and lack pride in their work. For a large proportion, English is their second language.
Stock market analysts	Want to provide analysis and reports which recommend a buy, hold or sell of specific house building company shares.
Prospective buyers	Want evidence from recent new home owners that their homes were fault-free on moving in.
New home owners	Want a fault-free house on Day 1 of moving in.
Official local planning officers	Want high financial contributions to other council services and a mix of private and social housing accommodation on new developments.
Building regulations officers	Want homes built to the specification that was approved.
Materials suppliers	Want early notification of specifications and quantities.
Environmentalists	Want minimum consumptions of water and energy.
Warranty providers	Want fewest faults possible, and no common trends.
Mortgage/home loan providers	Want an habitable home in order to advance the money to the buyer's solicitors.
Traditional media	Want personal stories from homeowners that are indicative of more widespread problems. Want distraught and emotional home owners' fiery complaints and photographs.
Social media	Photographs of snags and remedies that too went wrong, wants naming and shaming of companies and individuals.

Stage 2 – select target groups and individuals

UK Government	Establish the government department responsible for housing, the senior and junior ministers' contact details. Confirm the name and contact details of your local MP (or government representative).
House builders	Identify the trades' body and their contact details, the names of individual house builders, the names of the boards of directors and their contact details.
Sub-contractors	House builders don't build houses, their sub-contractors do. So tour the various housing developments near to you noting the company names from hi-vis jackets, vans, etc. Talk to individual tradespeople asking for company names. Compile a comprehensive list.
Tradespeople	An excellent source of inside information. Some are more open than others when asked about the development and the quality of work delivered. But silence too can be informative. Say that the conversation is 'off-the-record', and be specific with questions, e.g. 'What's being done well?' and, 'What could be done better?' 'Any problems/issues?'
Skills shortage/ apprentices	Often the sub-contractor will hire their own 'subbies'. Many may be unqualified casual workers, some paid on a daily basis. The quality of work is variable. Apprentices want to learn a trade and are more enthusiastic and committed to producing good work. Which minister is government is responsible for apprenticeships?
Stock market analysts	Identify the analysts by name and obtain contact details.
Prospective buyers	Unknown.
New home owners	Identify those who are willing to comment and be quoted.
Traditional media	Specific television programmes and their sub-contractors may be interested, as will named journalists. Find out who they are and their contact details.

Social media	There will be several pages that you can tap into. List them all.
Official local planning officers	Tend to quote official information, and not offer opinion.
Building regulations and officers	This is an interesting one as building companies have delegated powers to sign-off on new homes. One of the areas worth further exploration.
Materials suppliers	Under pressure from the builders to reduce costs. Worth noting the trade product names on site and searching online for the parent company and their contact details.
Environmentalists	A very powerful voice today and rightly so. The local authority will have people responsible. Contact details required.
Warranty providers	In the UK it's NHBC and Zurich. NHBC provide a ten-year warranty on new homes (for me, their reputation is poor).
Mortgage/home loan providers	Apparently their current test of whether to advance the money or not is to ask, 'Is the house habitable?' and not 'has the house been built to spec and does everything work?' or most appropriately, 'Would I be happy to move in here?'

Stage 3 – contact with them appealing to their agenda

Make contact with as many of the above list as possible and ask for their opinions about how well the current system works and where *they* would like to see improvements or changes. Their responses will either validate or alter the pre-judgements that you listed in Stage 1. For the above I would tell them all that I am campaigning for a better system under the alliterative banner – 'Faster Fault-free Freeholds'. Withhold your own detailed opinions at this stage as you may discover important information to fuel Stage 4 below.

Stage 4 – list your demands

From your own experiences and the input from Stage 3, construct a proposal that contains a series of options, ideally three or four, that range from minor adjustments to major change. Your proposal will have to include the people and organizations that you have contacted and their input. In your report show how their requirements will be addressed. People and organizations will have to opt to implement your proposal as legislative change is impossible. Can you create a logo or image that the interested parties can feature on their promotional efforts? That would make your scheme appear more 'official'. For example, commercial property constructors sign up to be 'Considerate Constructors'. Use any business case template from the internet as your rough proposal model, but you don't need to follow it slavishly. The executive summary should only be one A4 (8.5 by 11) page.

My options for the imagined house-building project may look something like this:

Option 1	The Council of Mortgage Lenders agrees to modify their sign-off criteria, establishing a stiffer inspection test.
Option 2	Option 1 plus House Builders consortium agrees to a new pre-completion home test by the site or project manager, which includes testing all water taps/showers/machines for leaks over a minimum of three hours and a full cycle functional test of all facilities.

Option 3	As Option 2 plus House Builders consortium agree to a 5 per cent retention by the buyer's solicitor of the monies payable on completion, which is released only when the buyer is satisfied with the snag corrections.
Option 4	As Option 3 plus the house builders consortium agrees to a new 'money back guarantee' if the new home owner rejects the property within seven days of moving in.

Stage 5 – negotiate changes and celebrate success, however limited

Steel yourself for the indifferent response to Stage 4. People and organizations don't like to change, so you will need to be patient. Concentrate your efforts on the one or two more enthusiastic avenues, the so-called 'early adopters'. Try to find the equivalent of Chapter 1's 'dancing man'. Aim to get one or two in agreement and others will follow, albeit reluctantly. The end result will almost certainly be a combination of both your ideas and the various stakeholders' ideas. Be flexible with what you include. Then celebrate your success, inviting journalists and local TV representatives to a briefing. Make sure you have a one-page summary available as a give-away.

Congratulations. You have led a project and influenced others around you to achieve your goal of building a house.

To start doing, you often need to stop

With a new to-do project, you will need to devote quite a lot of time to it, especially initially. Time that you currently spend doing other things. So you will need to stop doing some of the things that currently occupy your time. You will need to start a stop-doing list! And that statement hides another way for you to lead bigger groups and stakeholders. Just as the builders and the sub-contractors from our example above could stop doing stuff, so could many organizations, big and small. I'll give you two examples from my own experience.

First, when I was leading a sales and service organization in a large company, one of my duties was to complete a report on the activities, successes and failures of my group for the past month, and send it up the chain of command. One of the specific pre-ordained subjects was a win/loss report of significant sales. Once, I questioned my colleague who compiled the report for me from a variety of sources: 'Has anyone ever contacted us, asked any supplementary questions or made any observations on what we've sent?' 'No.' 'Then delete the win/loss report from now on and let's see what happens.' We did. And guess what? No one noticed.

The second example is from my time at the local hospital, where I help people with limited mobility on and off the courtesy bus, and take them from department to department around the huge campus. I noticed early on that the bus driver, a permanent employee, was required to enter every single trip 'from … to …' – several hundred yards at most. I asked whether anyone had commented on his log or asked any questions about it. 'No.' What is the purpose? If there is one, he hasn't been told.

Warren East at Rolls Royce has announced a series of lay-offs since he took post. Thousands of people have lost their jobs. It is unfortunately a consequence of poor past management but also part of the 'stop-doing' campaign he is leading the Company through. Their renaissance depends on focusing on what they do well, and doing that better. As a result some functions will be combined, some cut back either partially or entirely, and some outsourced. Leading the not doing is just as challenging, and still requires the same project template as start-doing.

Leading the customer with your reputation

Obviously one of the biggest groups of people that need to be engaged and led in business are called customers. We have referenced previously the CEOs of Lloyds Banking Group, Persimmon Homes and Rolls Royce. They each have a vision (what success looks like) of their future and a strategy (things to do to get there). Their customers have to be led to buy most products or services. But the question is how?

Companies put forward propositions to their target markets, and it turns out two of the main ingredients are reputation and track record. Academic research regularly tracks reputation of the world's leading companies and the relationship with sales success. Headhunters and recruiters generally track the same two subjects for individuals, and using that data create a shortlist of potential candidates for job vacancies. When you construct your CV/resumé, you list your achievements, your track record. Evidence of your leadership abilities are heavily weighted, even with highly specialized technical jobs. But your reputation is more difficult to establish, relying largely as it does, on the word of mouth of others.

Sir Philip Green is a British businessman, and the chairman of Arcadia Group, a retail company that includes Topshop. His name was recently revealed by a member of the House of Lords, in an extraordinary use of parliamentary privilege, as the person behind a *Daily Telegraph* investigation into abuse and harassment within his organization. Whether they are proved to be true or not, both his reputation and that of his company has been tarnished. Unfortunately for Sir Philip, his reputation had been previously damaged after selling another one of his companies, BHS, for £1 in 2015, which quickly went into administration with a pensions 'black hole' of over £500 million. Subsequently Sir Philip agreed, after pressure from the regulator, to pay £363 million into the BHS pension schemes.

Contrast how quickly Amazon founder Jeff Bezos responded when US Senator Bernie Sanders began excoriating Amazon for its low pay and poor working conditions of its warehouse workers. It is now paying all its workers a $15 dollar minimum starting wage and asking others to follow suit. 'You earn reputation by trying to do hard things well,' Bezos said to *BusinessWeek* back in 2004. 'People notice that over time.' And Bezos's strategy paid off: Amazon has consistently earned the highest overall ranking on the Harris Poll Reputation Quotient (RQ) study, which surveys 18,000 Americans to measure the reputations of the 60 most visible companies in the country.[2]

It doesn't matter how much money you may have – you can't buy a good reputation.

Final thoughts

So what do you think is your reputation? At home, in your local community, at work? What adjectives do others use when they talk about you?

Why am I asking? Because to lead and influence big groups and stakeholders, it is a huge advantage to have a reputation for getting things done. I bet you like to think that you enjoy a good reputation, don't you?

So, let's see. In Chapter 1, I asked you to collect input from others about where you set a good example and where you could set a better example. This next exercise is different in that it asks for adjectives that reflect your reputation. For the next two weeks, ask as many people as you can, to give you two adjectives that best describe your good points; your strengths; the qualities they like and admire about you. And two points that describe the areas that they think you could do better if you tried. Enter them here:

Positive adjectives	**More negative adjectives**

Even if you are elected as one of the leaders of your local toddler's playgroup, your local golf club, or appointed to lead one of the world's largest organizations, agreeing what success looks like with your colleagues and tabling a few options of how to get there is fundamental. We will discuss 'vision' later in Chapter 15. But there is very little difference between leading a child's play group and a large organization. Both are short of resources, both have demanding children/customers and both have to satisfy a wide audience of additional stakeholders. The scale is different, but the principles are the same. Good luck.

Question. List a couple of groups or organizations with whom you want to improve your relationship and another couple with whom you want to engage for the first time.

I want to improve my relationship with these	**I want to initiate a relationship with these**

The Everyday Leader-attempts to understand the 'stories' and core interests of those around them, and identifies commonalities with their own story for the future.
The Everyday Leader knows that a personal reputation for honesty and integrity can move others to act.

7

Leading thinking

This chapter acknowledges the importance of listening and observing, as first described in Chapter 2. It challenges readers to use the information they gather to think about the causes of things, to develop different scenarios of the future and to detail immediate actions that will prepare them for those possible futures. Now, if that all sounds a bit too abstract let's start with some examples.

Why are things the way they are?

Why do leading distance runners in the IAAF Diamond League[1] use pacesetters? Are they incapable of setting their own pace? Do they need shelter from the headwind on the back straight? Do they enjoy the close company of others? Do they enjoy chasing people? Have they been hypnotized to follow closely? Do they get lonely during a race and need company? And rather than being 'pulled along' why can't they be 'pushed along'? Why not have a pacesetter running from 'behind' and calling out the comparison between elapsed and target times? And does a new fastest time with a pacesetter break the previous record set without one?

As a fan of track and field, I need to know the answers! What do you think? Perhaps I need a pacesetter to write this book; perhaps we all need pacesetters in our daily lives?

And while I'm on the subject of sport, why are the Olympic Games treated as a contest between nations rather than athletes? Those nations that can afford to invest in the best training facilities and the best coaches tend to do better than those who can't. Why all the flag waving and national anthems? I'd like to see the athletes dressed identically with their national colours replaced by Olympic flags on their vests, sombre national anthems replaced by industrial-sized party poppers, showering the top five medal winners, not just three. What do you think?

Although I have chosen examples from athletics to pose the above questions, I could have chosen any 'norm' and questioned it. Why are we stuck with what we are stuck with? Maybe we are all so busy these days that we don't have time to think of the answers. But there are times in all our lives when we say to ourselves, 'I'd better sit down and have a think about this.' Teams need to think about how they can maximize their output. Organizations, both large and small, must constantly be in 'thinking mode' to avoid being overtaken by competitors and disruptors, and their products and services rendered obsolete.

So how do you go about thinking? What is the best model for you?

Modes of thinking

Management scholars have given names to many modes of thinking: 'blue sky', 'out of the box', etc. On a practical level, regardless of what they are called, I see three main objectives with any system designed to clarify our thinking:

1 *Thinking about the facts*, the data, the trends, and through understanding, make decisions.
2 *Thinking about the consequences* of tearing up the rule book when creating a new, superior methodology; and
3 *Thinking about risks* and through recognition and mitigation, limit potential losses.

Please allow me to describe briefly, three well-known and widely used thinking modes, namely *brainstorming, mind-mapping* and *six-thinking hats.*

Brainstorming: why it helps us overcome cognitive biases

Brainstorming is a particular way of generating lots of ideas. It is especially useful in situations when people are mentally 'stuck'. There is a problem in need of resolving and yet no one has any idea of how to proceed. Psychologists have a word for this situation: it's called *functional fixedness*. Functional fixedness, in a narrow sense, is our inability to see or use an object beyond its intended purpose (e.g., Do you throw out useful things because they are deemed to be 'garbage'? For example, my son threw out a pickle jar when the pickles were gone and then proceeded to buy a similar container from IKEA to hold sugar).

Famous Gestalt Psychologist Karl Duncker defined behaviour like this as emanating from a 'mental block against using [something] in a new way ... to solve a problem'. In a famous 1945 paper titled

'On Problem Solving', Duncker detailed a classic experiment demonstrating functional fixedness. Duncker gave his students a candle, a box of thumbtacks, and a book of matches, and asked them to attach the candle to the wall and light the wick so that the wax did not drip onto the table below. Duncker found that participants quickly became 'stuck' after trying such schemes as melting the wax and affixing the candle to the wall. Very few of them thought of the solution, which involves turning over the box of tacks and using the inside of the thumbtack box as a candle-holder, and tacking this to the wall. In Duncker's terms, the participants were 'fixated' on the box's normal function of holding thumbtacks and could not re-imagine it in a manner that could solve the problem.[2]

What helps participants overcome functional fixedness and arrive at better solutions to problems? Research has found that breaking up a problem into smaller bits and using collective wisdom to guide action can help greatly. We call this process 'brainstorming', and it can be staged in many different ways. In 'open outcry', for example, participants shout out their suggestions for one person to record on a chart or screen visible to all; or in a more closed environment, participants record their own ideas separately from each other on sticky labels before combining them on the same screen; or it can be a hybrid brainstorm, swapping between periods of noise and quiet, which is my personal recommendation.

This 'hybrid' brainstorming system starts with a burst of time-limited open outcry, say two minutes (where the extroverts dominate), followed by a quiet reflective period when individuals think alone (when the introverts blossom). Ideas can then be collected and recorded in turn, before starting the alternating system again, but this time with everyone stimulated by the thinking of others.

The objective of brainstorming is clear – to collect the highest number of ideas possible, irrespective of their advisability or viability. Everyone has to commit to quantity not quality in the early stages. Stupid, or plain crazy, suggestions are all equally valid in this stage of the exercise, and should be encouraged.

In Hollywood, they sometimes refer to this stage in idea generation as 'spitballing', a term made famous by screenwriter William Goldman,[3] who used it to describe getting together with another writer and discussing your script and coming up with ideas to solve problems with characters or plot. The first and only rule of spitballing, according to Goldman, was that there were no rules. Every idea – no matter how silly – should be entertained. The key, of course, is to allow some time for the good ideas to 'stick' and the poor ones to drop off.

So just like Goldman, it is important that *every* suggestion is greeted with complimentary comments such as 'Great idea Theresa,' 'Good one Boris.' And not 'Don't be daft Donald', or 'That won't work Nancy.' Judgement has to be suspended for the first phase of the exercise, otherwise too much time is spent dissecting each suggestion. And if suggestions are criticized, some people will feel too inhibited to offer more thoughts and ideas, fearing another slap-down.

The following are some of the widely accepted rules of brainstorming:

- Every person and every idea is equally valuable.
- Don't judge the ideas that others put forward, and don't let them judge yours.

- Encourage exaggerated and radical ideas.
- Go for volume of ideas – the quality doesn't matter initially.
- Build on the ideas of others – develop lots of combinations.

Eventually the flow of ideas dries up, in minutes usually, not hours, at which point we call a time-out, during which participants will start, automatically, to select their preferences. When together, you can split the group in two with one group prioritizing all the ideas, from the easy-to-implement to the most difficult, and the other group prioritizing from most radical or revolutionary to most standard or conventional. Place the two papers/flipcharts adjacent to each other and link them together – revolutionary and easy versus less radical and difficult. Everyone then takes a photo of the two charts and agrees to meet again after 24 hours, during which time they each individually decide on their top three choices. General discussion follows and decisions are made.

If you haven't tried it before, or want to get the group in the right frame of mind, then try a simple exercise such as, 'Let's think of 50 different uses for a camel. I'll start – how about milking!'

Mind-mapping: visualizing ideas makes a big difference

Mind-mapping is another well-known management technique for clarifying thinking that can be used in your daily life as well as in combination with brainstorming. For example: let's suppose that you are a parent and that one of your children has passed an important milestone, an exam, or their driving test, and you want to celebrate their success. You and your partner think of a number of attractive but random options, before organizing them into specific groups. You do this automatically and without too much thought. In your mind the options look like this:

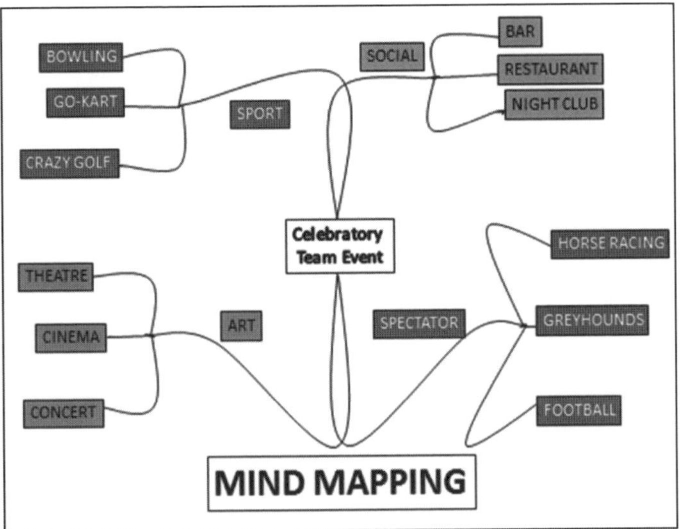

You may select one particular event or choose one from each group: concert then restaurant. Done! But with more complex challenges, visualizing the choices via mind mapping can play a very helpful role, especially in negotiations. For Brexit in the UK, re-label 'sport, social, art and spectator' as 'customs and excise, immigration, law making and citizens rights'. In the US, re-label as 'border control, healthcare, taxation and rust-belt regeneration'. To secure your preference in one area you may agree to give way in another. I've used it inside and outside boardrooms, and it works.

We all have a way of thinking that is unique to us: the six 'thinking hats' approach

By bringing people together, brainstorming and mind-mapping have the obvious benefit of securing a wide range of opinions, prejudices and tolerances. Everyone has their preferred way of thinking. No one thinks like you do, no one thinks like I do. We are all different. And yet, the great management expert Edward de Bono has developed a system of detailed and coherent thinking for groups of people both large and small, which can assimilate these differences. Published in 1985, his book *Six Thinking Hats* allocates a specific way of thinking to roleplay with six different colours. I have used his method countless times and recommend it to you.

De Bono asks you to force your brain to think about a question or issue from a series of quite specific and in many ways, unnatural, viewpoints. For example, if you are a 'glass half-full person', or a 'glass half-empty person' you will be stimulated to think from the opposite point of view, as well as your most natural. *Why?* Because most people have a propensity to think in the same, or a similar way, about each and every challenge. De Bono offers an alternative that encourages people to think differently and thoroughly. Here are the colours and the thinking they represent reproduced with permission from www.debono.com:

The **White Hat** calls for information known or needed. 'The facts, just the facts.'

The **Yellow Hat** symbolizes brightness and optimism. Under this hat you explore the positives and probe for value and benefit.

The **Black Hat** is judgement – the devil's advocate or why something may not work. Spot the difficulties and dangers; where things might go wrong. It's probably the most powerful and useful of the Hats but a problem if overused.

The **Red Hat** signifies feelings, hunches and intuition. When using this hat you can express emotions and feelings and share fears, likes, dislikes, loves and hates.

The **Green Hat** focuses on creativity; the possibilities, alternatives and new ideas. It's an opportunity to express new concepts and new perceptions.

The **Blue Hat** is used to manage the thinking process. It's the control mechanism that ensures the Six Thinking Hats® guidelines are observed.

Try it out with your colleagues, friends or family to get the feel for it using a challenge such as, 'Where shall we all go for a holiday next year?' At work you may experiment with a trial such as, 'In the next 45 minutes we are going to re-design our company's logo symbol and strapline.' I usually start with the black hat – to discover what's wrong with what we have, or what we did. But don't spend too long in each hat as your brain will have a tendency to revert to its normal way of thinking and you'll lose the benefit.

I had the pleasure of observing Edward de Bono at the London School of Economics in 2009, when he demonstrated his model and engaged the entire audience of about 1,000 to participate fully in providing a response to this statement, 'Having caused the financial global meltdown in 2008, bankers' bonuses should be more heavily taxed'. Initially the vast majority were in favour, but after he took the audience through his model in about 30–40 minutes in total, the outcome was different. *Why?* Because he forced people to think thoroughly and without prejudice or pre-conception.

He started his session with seemingly simple question, 'Please add the numbers 1 to 10 together. What's the total?' Within a few seconds there were shouts of 55. 'Well done,' he said, 'Now add the numbers 1 to 200 together, what's the answer?' Laughter for several seconds until someone shouted the correct answer, 20, 100. 'Correct', he said. Then he explained why he had asked the questions. 'With the first question, you probably all started with 1 and then added 2 to make 3 and then added 4 to make 7 etc., until you reached 55. But that is only one way to get the right answer. You could have multiplied 10 by 11 and divided the answer by 2 to get to 55 via a different thought process. 200 multiplied 201 divided by 2 is still a calculation that is possible to undertake without the use of a calculator, and get to the answer of 20,100 pretty quickly.'

He was showing his audience an example of situations where there is more than one way to tackle a problem, if you go and look for it. Different thinking. He says that many people have a tendency to stick with the way they have previously approached a problem, without giving themselves, or others, the time to think of possible alternatives or a new way forward. De Bono says that it's important when using the thinking hats in a group, that everyone uses the same hat or thinking style at least once. It's not about personal preferences but more about encouraging parallel thinking, a collaborative, exploratory approach, rather than 'I am right, you are wrong'.

Can you identify the best way forward to address a problem or current issue by using the 'Six Thinking Hats' methodology? Almost certainly. And you'll have fun doing it! Good luck.

Accounting for and accommodating individual differences

In the three thinking models above, the thinking is done in groups. So if you have a particular issue or personal problem that you need to tackle, these models argue that it's best to share it and co-opt others to help you. The challenge that you face has been faced before by thousands, if not millions, of people. If you're feeling lonely, unloved, isolated or simply 'down', try to remember that help is possibly only a few doors down (if you are at work) or just a few clicks away (if you are sitting at home in front of the computer). Find a group (virtual or real) and join it. If your team or organization is in a downward spiral, join the club. Literally! Communicating with others who have the same issue and those that don't, may spark the realization of a way forward.

For some people, asking for help may seem like an admission of failure, inadequacy or guilt. As the everyday leader you must talk openly about this tendency, and translate any request for help to be an act of bravery.

When you organize your next 'thinking workshop', please remember to also include members who have different mind-sets and customs. Christians worship on a Sunday, Jews on a Saturday, and Muslims on a Friday. There are meat-eaters, vegetarians and vegans. Dancing is a celebration for some and sacrilegious to others. Two people holding hands in the street can be the custom, or the cause of quizzical looks. Different sexual orientations are accepted by some and considered immoral by others. Trans-gender issues have challenged even the most progressive institutions in recent years.

My point is, in our new globalized and pluralistic world, there is no universally accepted 'norm' or 'standard' that we can assume an audience will follow. There is no normal or abnormal; there is no natural or unnatural; there is no usual or unusual. Which is why you need to get a range of people to your workshops: organize a student exchange for the summer vacation; holiday with a local family and immerse yourself in a different culture; appoint a teenager and a senior citizen to your governing board of directors.

What to think about?

So now that you have been exposed to some basic models of how to organize your thinking, what will you think about? What are the issues that demand some serious thinking from you and about your family, your friends; your community; for your work team?

When kids are young, parents start to imagine the world in which they will grow up; parents think about education and costs, medical insurance, geographic location for opportunities; personal and environmental safety; relationships with the extended family, etc. When today's parents were kids there was no Uber, Facebook, Alibaba or Airbnb and yet in less than a generation they have become ubiquitous. As artificial intelligence, robotics and machine learning develop according to Moore's Law,[4] they will rob great swathes of white-collar professionals of their jobs. Middle-class labour market opportunities are under increasing attack in the twenty-first century like never before. Have you planned for being out of work? How long would you survive without being forced to make significant changes to your family's way of life?

How will the everyday leaders of today (teachers, CEOs, managers, parents etc.) ensure the prosperity of their students, citizens, workers, customers, or their kids? More specifically – what are *you* going to do? How do you talk with your kids, what do you discuss; how do you collect their thoughts and interpret their behaviour? And are you prepared to make sacrifices to *your* way of life to ensure *their* success/survival? These are questions that we all need to start thinking about.

If you are troubled with a particular problem or opportunity, and thinking about the subject disturbs your sleep, then make sure you have a notepad and pencil on your bedside table. During 'rapid eye movement' (REM) sleep, the brain automatically tries to make sense of the inputs it has taken in, and may organize an answer to the problem for you sub-consciously. How often have you heard the phrase, 'I was lying in bed when the solution suddenly popped into my head'? Apparently some musicians hear fully formed tunes in their dreams, or reorganize the notes they were playing yesterday into a new blockbuster. It has been widely reported that when Paul McCartney heard his mother Mary's voice (who had recently died) in a dream, he awoke one morning, sat down at the keyboard and immediately played an entirely new tune. *Let it Be* was born. Other musicians have reportedly had similar experiences,[5] so maybe you will too. The *eureka* moment for you may come from your dreams, from serendipity, from a quick brainstorming session or it may be developed during an in-depth workshop.

Making the future part of your current thinking

In Chapter 2, I offered the acronym PESTLE, often used in business planning, as being useful for personal planning purposes as well. What are the trends that *will* affect your future; that *may* affect your future; and where is the unit or team vulnerable to unknown surprises that may threaten their survival?

You may have heard of the term 'scenario planning', which is simply a way of describing firstly, the search for the two most important factors that will impact your future viability; secondly to show how the degree to which they may apply will affect your performance; and thirdly to start preparation for those eventualities. It's less about thinking of changes to population or GDP, and more about thinking about the possible disrupters, the sudden and unexpected change of methodology, and rapid technology developments that may make your systems obsolete. We call these 'Black Swan' events, aptly described as such by former options trader Nassim Nicholas Taleb in his prescient 2007 book *The Black Swan: The Impact of the Highly Improbable*. The book focuses on the extreme impact of rare and unpredictable outlier events (such as spotting a 'black swan'); and the human tendency to find simplistic explanations for these events, retrospectively. Taleb calls this the Black Swan theory and recommends a different way of thinking of the world as a set of interconnected actors working inside different but interrelated 'systems'.

Systems thinking (ST) is therefore another term with which you should become familiar. In ST, instead of breaking down an individual process or processes into a sequential series of activities or operations, workshops examine the process within the context of the other processes within the overall system. ST attempts to identify the consequences and knock-on effects of making changes to one system within the complexity of a multi-system design, before attempting to compensate for them, knowing that the compensations will, in themselves, have knock-on effects, both known and unknown.

If we look at a national education system, for example, you can imagine that it contains many sub-systems: government policy; student selection; curricular and timetables; teaching methodology; examination measurements; pastoral care; discipline and punishment. I won't go on, but you immediately realize that changes to one element of the overall system will impact others, both knowingly and unknowingly. For every action there is an equal and opposite reaction, said Newton. At home, restricting your child to a time limit with their tablets may encourage them to visit their friend's house more often where you are not able to police them; a favourite of mine at work is when teams or organizations attempt to increase sales. Some bright spark will at some stage ask, 'What is the definition of a sale?' Soon fictitious sales will be recorded, sales between subsidiaries will rise, friendly customers will place orders in one accounting period for them to be cancelled the next. When this fraud is uncovered, as it usually is, then sales drop, frequently lower than the original level through reputation damage. A rigorous and intense ST examination can often identify these potential pitfalls early.

Final Thoughts

So when are you next going to stop and think? What will you think about? How will you think? Who will you think with? How much time will you devote to thinking? And will you try to improve the quality and results of thinking in your family, your team and your organization? But caution is needed before accessing the digital media world to help or stimulate your thinking. It may limit inadvertently your abilities to think abstractedly about the bigger picture. In a study completed by Dartmouth College[6] they found that a broader understanding of a situation was achieved when the data was presented in a non-digital form (e.g. printed format) when compare to a digital form (e.g. on a laptop). So when the problem or challenge doesn't have a concrete answer, it may be best to disconnect yourself (and others) from the incessant noise of the everyday (phones and computers) giving yourself time and space, even by physical separation, in order to reflect and prioritize. I wish you well.

Question. You have to, or will have to, make decisions about the following subjects at home, in your community and at work. List them and share your answers with others. Discussions, meetings and/or workshops will follow.

Decisions needed at home	**Decisions needed with friends**	**Decisions needed at work**

The Everyday Leader thinks more about tomorrow than today and identifies the most important factors for survival and future success.
The Everyday Leader doesn't assume that what they have today will survive the challenges of tomorrow.

8

Leading relationships

Social ties are the bedrock of human existence and everyday leadership is built on the cultivation and maintenance of relations with others. This chapter offers guidance on how to foster and improve personal relationships at home, at work and in the community.

Emotional intelligence '101'

A taxi driver I used frequently to get to and from the airport was also the personal driver of a director of a large well-known company. I asked him how the director, Myra (not her real name), was getting on, and he replied: 'She is the most stupid clever person, I've ever met.' He meant that she was a terrific conceptualizer and planner, but was lacking in the ability to 'read' the mood and emotional state of the people around her. Her words and demeanour sometimes didn't 'fit' with the situations she encountered. She lacked emotional intelligence.

The term emotional intelligence (EI) was virtually unknown prior to 1995, when journalist and science writer Daniel Goleman published his bestselling book *Emotional Intelligence: Why it Can Matter More than IQ*.[1] But today an unfiltered Google search reveals 165 million entries! And yet, despite its ubiquity and popular usage, it's still not a well-practiced concept. EI, in its simplest form, describes the capability of individuals to recognize their own emotions and to respond to them with conscious self-reflection, 'I'm getting angry now, I'd better calm down', and also to recognize the emotional state of others and respond appropriately. People with a well-developed ability to empathize with others are said to enjoy high emotional intelligence (or a high EQ). They can sense how a person or a group feels, re-create the same feelings in themselves, and reply with the most appropriate facial expression, words and/or tone that they themselves would acknowledge as kind and understanding in the same situation.

Unfortunately, Myra – though brilliant in the many technical aspects of her job – couldn't empathize. She couldn't look at someone and be able to sense their mood. She wouldn't adjust her expression or her tone of voice to suit the occasion. And more, she didn't believe that anything was amiss. She would never say, 'You seem a little quiet, everything OK?' because her emotional radar would never have detected it. Myra had a big social disadvantage and didn't even realize it. Emotional intelligence is difficult to coach, it's difficult to teach, but it's not impossible. By consciously leveraging your emotional intelligence, you will be better able to establish and maintain relationships with your extended family, neighbours and colleagues at work.

There's a Haribo advert on TV promoting its range of chewy sweets for kids. It features a group of serious-looking adults, either waiting on a station platform or in an elevator, who suddenly and unexpectedly start talking to each other excitedly, and with an incongruous young child's voice, about the merits of the individual sweet designs. If this had been a real event, those with high emotional intelligence would perhaps have adopted the same childish voice and extolled the virtues of competitor Maynard's Wine Gums.

Seeing is believing . . . in others

Members of the northern Natal tribes of South Africa greet one another daily by saying 'Sawubona', which literally means: 'I see you.' The response is 'Sikhona' which means: 'I am here'. This exchange is important, for it denotes that 'until you "see" me, I do not exist; and when you "see" me, you bring me into existence.'

Roland Sinker, the chief executive of Addenbrooke's Hospital in Cambridge said to me, 'I have to keep my feet on the ground, and my eyes on the stars.' Keeping his feet on the ground by, for example, completing a full shift as a porter, moving bed-bound patients around wards and departments. He learns a lot when he takes on the roles of his employees: 'I was invisible to everyone,' he said to me. 'Nobody "saw" me.'

I noticed that when the Pope boards his Alitalia flight from Rome, the two guards of honour at the foot of the aircraft steps come to attention and salute the Pontiff. His Holiness 'sees' them and offers his hand in friendship. The guards have to relax their bodies, become less rigid, and lower their arms in order to shake his hand and smile, before resuming their smart formality. Contrast the Pope's response to those around him with the US President who usually salutes the two Marines at the foot of the helicopter's steps, but never extends a hand

and thereby passes on the opportunity to 'see' them as real people, and not just a uniform or performance extra.

How many people have you 'seen' today? And how many have you not seen? Seeing the person and trying to understand their 'story', is essential if you are going to ask them to develop a relationship with you, which is strong enough for them to be motivated to follow you. You have to tap into their world, identify their many needs and then link them to yours.

The 'social ties' that bind

Social scientists have been able to quantify the 'cost' to individuals and society of not reaching out and forming even the most casual of social relationships. It turns out our social ties, whether weak or strong, confer benefits beyond the purely emotional, though that's important too. Think of how you use your social media accounts, LinkedIn or Facebook for example. Are all of your relationships examples of a 'strong tie' in that you count all of your connections as close personal friends? Or are they former colleagues that you might like very much but who you only occasionally interact with? Are the ties equally important to you? Should they be? The answer turns out to be, 'yes'.

Mark Granovetter, a sociologist whose work identified the power of social ties long before social networks proliferated on the internet, refers to how interpersonal relationships between different, disparate groups of people can hold people and even different sections of society together. In Granovetter's model, 'strong' and 'weak' tie relationships in our social networks are equally important but fulfil different roles.[2] Strong ties provide you with financial, moral and psychological support when you need it the most. They foster trust. Weak ties by contrast have been found to spread crucial information about new job opportunities, and new customers for your business, big or small. Let's look at a few examples.

Imagine that you are a high-powered technology expert, in demand all over the world for your IT skills. Now think about a couple of your friends that you grew up with, who understand technology but you wouldn't class as techno-geeks. They have interests in other areas and are on the edge of your closest circle of present-day friends (i.e. they are an example of your 'weak ties'). However, these weak ties are crucial in binding groups of strong ties together. They bring circles of networks into contact with each other, strengthening relationships and forming new bonds between existing relationships. Your childhood friends might have information that is mutually beneficial to you and them, but more importantly, these ties encourage sharing of information across different groups.

Let's say I lived in a socially cohesive group consisting almost entirely of Arsenal Football fans. (Actually that could be true!) I would never get any information from the West Ham fans at the edges of my network, as I only communicated with my fellow Arsenal fans (i.e., my 'strong ties'). I might miss the announcement that a reunion-charity match between London's greatest footballers was to be played at the London Stadium in a week's time (West Ham's home park) and tickets were still available. Focusing entirely on my Arsenal crowd means I'd miss the opportunity enjoyed by all of my football-loving weak ties. You get the idea.

Perhaps it's time to get in touch with some of your former acquaintances and see what you've been missing.

'Ask' and you shall receive . . . a stronger relationship

Last week, I had a new crew-mate in my hospital courtesy bus, someone who I had never met. We were going to be together for a few hours. We could have done our own jobs and departed the same strangers as when we had met. Instead, when we had a moment without any passengers, I asked her to tell me her life story in five minutes. I was stunned by her first statement, 'I had a bad childhood, was homeless for a while, but still managed to complete my studies and pass my exams at 18 years old.' Gradually over the next few hours, I discovered that she was a victim of physical violence, first at the hands of her biological father, and then by her step-dad, before the step-dad evicted her forcibly from her own home at age 14. She had tried to join the Royal Navy a few years later, but was unlucky as she had a temporary medical condition, and the Navy would not hold open a provisional place for her condition to clear. She never mentioned a partner. I guess many relationships are understandably tainted by her upbringing. I learnt that she housed a menagerie of animals, from cats and dogs to chickens and guinea pigs. She clearly has the potential to do more than drive a small bus, and I encouraged her to do so, but the world must wait for the future chapters of her story to be written.

Had we been afforded the time during that conversation, I'm sure she would have asked me to tell her about the story of my life. But we haven't been rostered on the same shift since, or she may have taken another job somewhere else. I mention this because it is important when building and leading relationships that stories need to be exchanged and regularly updated. How many times have you been bored by, and subsequently avoided, someone who talks only about themselves and forgets to ask you about your day?

How good are you at listening? Could you do better? How good a listener are you with those around you, your family, your work colleagues? How good are you at responding in kind and asking others how they are doing? Try and encourage people to open up and maybe acknowledge, if you have the trust of those around you, that reciprocating and offering up opportunities for listening to the concerns of others is an essential part of being an everyday leader in life as in work. From my acquaintance on the bus, unloved and abused in childhood, to married adults who manage and maintain the most important relationship in their lives, the one they have with their partner. Often communicating without words, speaking without talking, and messaging with their eyes and hands. When discussing emotional intelligence, perhaps this is the highest level of performance that we can attain as individuals. So 'in tune' with our partner's thought processes that we finish their sentences; so 'in tune' with our partner's moods that we unknowingly and automatically adjust our own responses in word and deed, so that they 'fit' the situation.

Forge relationships with those who are least like you

So, armed with the knowledge that to enjoy long-lasting and successful interpersonal relationships, your focus needs to be on the other party, I'm going to ask you to react to the following scenario:

You are on holiday, relaxing by the pool on a sun lounger about to read a book. Lucky you. I want you for a moment, irrespective of your true nature, to regard yourself as a huntin'/shootin'/fishin' outdoor type of person, an extrovert, an alpha personality.

You put your book down to wipe your face and turn to the stranger on your left. 'It's a warm one, alright!' The conversation starts and you soon discover that she's convalescing and rarely sits by any pool. 'Poolside is not really me,' she says, 'I'm a huntin'/shootin'/fishin' outdoor type of person, some call me an alpha female.' You spend the rest of the day swapping experiences, laughing a lot, and drinking more than you should. How about that, you stumbled upon someone who is exactly like you!

Without her the following day, you get back to your book. After a quick dip, you find a newcomer on the lounger next to you. 'Hello. How are you today?', and the conversation begins. You discover that much like the 1990s Radiohead song, he likes a quiet life with no surprises. 'I always come back to this hotel for a week every year,' he says. 'I'm a person of habit and quite shy really. I'm not really one of those people who want to go exploring different countries, or seeking fresh challenges. I like my home life exactly as I have it.'

The following morning by the poolside, there are empty loungers on either side of you. You look around to see if either of your two new lounger buddies will join you, hoping that one of them will.

Is your preference for the extrovert, outdoors person, or the more introverted person of habit? Be honest. It's the person most like the imaginary you, right? You wouldn't be alone. My guess is that most people would choose to spend their time with people of the same ilk, missing out on the opportunity to forge new relationships with different 'ilks'. But as an everyday leader, I would advise you to initiate, develop and maintain relationships with as wide a personal network as possible, prioritizing those who hold different viewpoints to yourself. If you accept the recommendation you will be challenged to identify one or more common threads that could bind you together if the need arises.

As Mark Granovetter and the sociology of weak ties shows, the personal networks of everyday leaders should contain a constantly refreshed and rejuvenated multi-coloured rainbow of contacts. Don't stick with what you've always stuck.

Refresh and rework your relationships

In Chapter 2 Tony Ryan and Michael O'Leary examined the status quo of the airline industry and ripped it apart. When you look at the relationships in your own family, stand back occasionally, but regularly, and look at the status quo of your family unit. As everyone gets older, relationships need to change.

So what do you see? How well is your model working? And how do you believe that an independent observer or counsellor would report on the efficiency and effectiveness of the way your unit operates; how much love and support do each of the family members enjoy and do these need to change (some requiring more, while others less)? How would your family assess your contributions and the way that you lead? How do your family members rank your ability to lead them? If asked, what would they like you to change? And if they asked you the same question, what would you like them to change?

Name of individual	They say I set a good example with this	They would like me to improve with this	I would like them to do more of this	I would like them to do improve with this
Partner				
Child				
Child				
Child				

If you are experiencing problems with your partner, simply talking through the issue quietly and calmly may improve things instantly. Always talk about your own feelings with your partner's behaviour by starting with, 'I feel . . . [sad, annoyed, frustrated, etc.] by your . . . when you . . . etc.'

Why is it important to start a sentence this way? Because feelings are subjective and unique to you. No one can say 'No, you don't feel that way!' By contrast, if you start with a statement with, 'You never . . . [empty the dishwasher, walk the dog, clean the car etc.], you create the potential for argument: 'That's not true, I walked the dog only yesterday!'

From home to work, unsurprisingly, the challenges and opportunities are similar. Is your team at work under threat of re-organization? Are people leaving in fear of upcoming redundancy rumours? Are your targets achieved well ahead of time? Does your opinion count? Is the bigger picture sustainable? Does your company pay its invoices on time? Do you feel under pressure, or worse, is work making you feel a little depressed?

Instead of waiting for the independent observer to conduct a survey or audit, you may wish to consider taking up the role for yourself, involving others in the process of course. You have the opportunity to lead. Will you take it?

Name of team member	They say I set a good example with this	They would like me to improve with this	I would like them to do more of this	I would like them to improve with this
Team member				
Team member				
Team member				
Team member				

The employment relationship

There is one other relationship I wish to explore, and that is between manager and worker. And from both perspectives, using the same four questions from the above examples. You will be able to complete the following grid immediately:

	They say I set a good example with this	They would like me to improve with this	I would like them to do more of this	I would like them to improve with this
Manager				
Worker				

Recognizing the differences among cultures, most managers/bosses will be happy to discuss this with you. Maybe they already have, and if so, I hope that they have told you about the subjects in columns 2 and 3 during your regular appraisals. Annual appraisals, by the way, are so yesterday. Monthly is the new model, but conducted more informally. The best boss I ever had, met with me monthly in a wine bar, discussed my performance in the round and then asked me for my opinion not only on how he performed for me, but also on the future plans he was thinking about. I felt involved. And I guess that's the test, isn't it. Do you feel involved?

If your boss has not requested feedback on their leadership and management performance, then may I suggest that you show them this chapter, pointing directly to the grid above; ask for comments on what you have inserted in columns 1 and 2; and be ready to respond when he or she reads what you have entered in columns 3 and 4. I hope it starts a productive and interesting exchange.

The case of the 'insensitive boss'

I have enjoyed the pleasure and privilege of helping many people at all levels in organizations, more often in large multi-national organizations. All coaching exchanges are private and confidential of course, so the following story is a combination of the many people I have met and coached over the years.

Let's call our leader Felix. He is in his late thirties, highly competitive and very results-oriented. But he has an issue that has bugged him for some time. Occasionally when responding to a question or statement, the words he chooses come across as brutally insensitive and disrespectful – dismissive even – which some observers called, inaccurately, arrogant. He regrets that, at times, his behaviour at home can be similar. But he doesn't mean to be brutal and he is not arrogant. Being highly self-analytical he has determined that he is most likely to respond like this when under increased pressure and, unusually, also when he is under almost zero pressure.

As he is an athlete I ask Felix if he has ever worn his heart monitor at work and tried to correlate the times when he regretted his verbal reactions to the physical indicators on his monitor. He said he had but there was no correlation. I tell him that this doesn't appear correct, as increased pressure would, generally, tend to cause the heart to beat faster. We discuss this and he says that he will repeat the recordings over a longer period and report back. In the meantime I recommend that he reads a couple of books which I think may help him.

During our next discussion, I ask him about how his sports performances were judged by his coaches, as I suspect that he has become desensitized to harsh criticism and learned to give as good as he gets. 'Just the opposite,' he says. 'My coaches were supportive and generous.'

Another road closed.

Eventually, I urge him to think about trialling a coloured card system together with his family and colleagues. I suggest to him that he might 'come clean' and admit his battle to do better to his family and work colleagues, and ask for their support. I suggest that he distribute two differently coloured cards during exchanges and discussions, so when anyone is offended by his remarks, he would ask them to raise, for example, a yellow card, representing, 'I'm a bit sore after that comment or statement.' Just like a football referee, no words would be needed. But, to recognize when he makes progress and refrains from insensitive comments, his audience should raise, for example, a blue card to represent, 'Well done for using more agreeable and acceptable language and comment.' I further suggest that Felix consider letting everyone else use the cards system with their colleagues and at any time. After much thought, he experiments with the cards, but dispenses with them, as everyone quickly became comfortable with using the word, 'Ow!' and a thumbs-up instead. Progress.

Relations between organizations

Leading relationships between and with other organizations demands a systematic approach where policy is, and standard operating procedures are, clearly defined, promulgated, and followed by all parties. Small organizations are compelled to adhere to larger companies' terms and conditions, and yet I have found often that the larger organization doesn't follow their own payment terms, leaving the smaller party strapped for cash. The smaller organization is powerless in these circumstances, as they may depend on future orders from the same large organization for their survival. Although the larger firm can pride itself on its tight financial management discipline, the effects on supply chain relationships can be devastating.

During the past ten years or so, contractual payment terms have been increased, leading to even greater pressure on smaller suppliers. Three- and four-month payment terms are common in many multi-national corporations' contracts these days. Is it fair? No. Does the practice damage relationships? Yes. But there is hope. The UK supermarket chain Waitrose moved its payment terms for all UK small food producers, whose business with the retailer is worth less than £100,000 annually, to a maximum of seven days.[3] That is a sure way to improve supplier–retailer relations. And if you work in or around the supply chain, maybe you could examine the terms and conditions of your own organization and see if there is room for improvement. Is there an opportunity for an everyday leader like you?

Question. You decide to improve your relationship with someone at home, one of your friends, and a group of people at work. What are your options?

Name of person at home	**Name of friend**	**Name of group**
Options		

The Everyday Leader regularly touches base with others in their network to ask how they are without having a reason other than to do so.
The Everyday Leader never forgets to acknowledge the doorkeeper, receptionist or server properly.

9

Leading from a distance

This chapter tackles the difficulties and challenges involved in leading those who are far from home, working geographically at a distance or in a different time zone (for example, a teenager backpacking around Asia or a worker offshore on an oil rig).

The 'hologram' version of you

Let's begin with the objective of leading from a distance. The task for you as the everyday leader is to create in the mind of your distant family members or workers, an imaginary hologram of you that sits or walks with them every day, and the image is so strong that they know how you would react in any given circumstance, even if you are not physically there. They should know the strength of feeling that you would have because they know your values and ethics. They need to know what kind of person you are.

It would be fantastic if they not only knew but also *identified* with your values and ethics, as it would make their judgements easier, but that is not a prerequisite. What really matters is that they know your 'story', warts and all. Once you have established the imaginary hologram, regular maintenance and polishing will keep it vivid in the minds of distant souls. And it goes without saying that they need to know their own goals and the team's goals; the initiatives to reach them; their specific responsibilities; who relies and depends upon on the distant team's output; and the critical timelines.

So open, honest and close communication is vital. If the left hand doesn't know what the right hand is doing it can't help, nor can it adjust its own behaviour and actions in the light of the information being denied to it.

Maintain constant and clear communication

How many times have you been in these situations and heard the following?

'Jane has just called. She wants to be picked up from the station. I thought you said you were going to pick her up when we spoke this morning.' Your response, 'Sorry I got delayed and forgot all about it.'

'At our last team meeting you said you were going to ask Manuel's team for help, but when I spoke to Manuel earlier he said he knew nothing about it. What do you want me to do?'

Keep all team members in close communication. Use technology – shared sites, video, common platforms/software – and communicate in clearly understood language, avoiding jargon whenever you can. Spades need to be called 'spades' and not 'digging solutions'.

It always surprises me when those high up in organizations feel the need to disguise the meaning of their message with so-called 'management speak', which very few can translate into something meaningful. Helen Cahill interviewed Joe Gordon, the CEO of UK bank First Direct in October 2018 for the *Mail on Sunday* and found him 'surprisingly hard to understand'. In her article she prepared the following table to illustrate her point:

But he can't stop speaking in jargon – so here's what it really means	
WHAT HE SAYS	**WHAT IT MEANS**
'Provisioning journey'	How the bank responds to a customer request or complaint
'Busting the stress of choice'	The bank recommending products that save customers the time and hassle searching for a good deal
'Disruption curve'	The number of companies offering a new type of product or service and how widely available it is
'The service–relationship space'	Customer service
'Transactional trust'	Whether customers trust banks when they hand over money
'The hygiene of digital'	Keeping customers' money safe online, for example by having strong passwords and identity checks
'Disintermediating utility providers'	Taking over the job of selling gas and electricity so power firms no longer sell directly to households
'Customer contact environment'	Call centre

Understanding your story and theirs

In the process of asking your distant family members or work colleagues to understand your story, you will gain an understanding of theirs. You will discover that some might welcome the distance between you, while others will need to feel closer.

When I was working for the big corporates, I was exposed to different types of leadership, from micromanagement to hands-off. No one ever asked me what kind of leadership and management brought the best out of me. If they had, I would have told them that I preferred to be left to my own devices.

Have you asked those closest to you if the way you treat them is the way in which *they prefer* to be treated? Does your leadership style bring out the best in them? If not, then you're the one who needs to change, not them.

Let's think of a family member about to embark on a long solo business trip, or your backpacking teenager and your worries primarily about their safety, and whilst we're doing that try to think about your distant workers in the same light. First of all, can your emotional intelligence put you in their shoes in order to see the world from their perspective? Do you know the story, some elements perhaps unspoken, of your teenager? You might think you know of their hopes and fears; their level of self-confidence; what attracts them and what repulses them. You think you know how they will react in different situations, to various threats, opportunities, peer pressure, and to authority. You are pretty sure you know why they want to go on this trip and who they are going with. But most of all you worry about their level of naivety, their lack of worldliness. They don't have your level of suspicion or cynicism. And they don't have your high level of sensitivity to potential risk.

They are now been away for more than a month and you prepare for the first monthly Skype call – what will you say? And most importantly, how will you try to discover the truth about how they really feel? After all, they are intelligent enough to know that you will worry about them, and they will try to gloss over the stuff that they think will worry you more. So you consider the usual slate of questions:

Home	**Work**
'How are you?'	*'How are you?'*
'Where are you?	*'Where are you with your projects/milestones?*
'How are those with you?'	*'How are your colleagues? 'Are you getting enough cooperation?'*
'What's been good?'	*'Tell me about the stuff that's going well?'*
'What are you doing next?'	*'So what's happening over the next couple of weeks?'*

This is all good, but now think about the negative stories they are occulting and how your questions may be reframed to help them really open up to you. So, as they tell you their story so far, it's time to pick up on the potential negatives:

Home	**Work**
'What has been the worst thing that's happened?' 'It must have been awful!'	'What has been the most serious disappointment so far?'
'What else was bad?'	'I bet it didn't stop there – bad news comes in three's. What else failed?'
'You must have felt hurt!' 'It must have been difficult to recover?'	'How has the customer and the project team reacted?'
'I bet you're ready to come home, aren't you?'	'Will you have a serious think about whether we revise times and costs, or even whether we should close this thing down completely?'
'So what lessons have you learned so far that you could pass on to those that follow in your footsteps?'	'So what lessons have you and the team learned that you believe would help other project teams?'

My wife's sister Betty passed away in 2016, after spending about four months in hospital. The hospital was 200 miles from our home and about four hours travel time. A day visit was unrealistic, so we stayed overnight in a local hotel every three to four weeks. In between, my wife telephoned the hospital to see how Betty was doing. A security code was set up so that the hospital staff had the authority from Betty to tell my wife the accurate detail of Betty's condition. But my wife still had to lead the conversation and the nurses' reluctant negativity: So questions like: 'I bet she hasn't been feeding herself yet?' 'Still bed-bound, I suppose?' 'What are the doctors most concerned about?' did more to lead the nurses to open up than, 'How is Betty today?'

It's hard to press for the true story, especially when it's mostly negative, but it helps avoid informational bombshells. Had my wife not been adamant that she know the true extent of her sister's illness, the pain of coming to terms with her death, in such a short period of time (a mere four months), would have been far worse.

Avoiding broken telephones in the age of teleconferencing

We have so many technologies that facilitate communicating at a distance, and yet miscommunication is common, in families, in teams and especially in organizations. It means we are failing to communicate our ideas or intentions successfully. Without those interpersonal face-to-face interactions, it is extremely difficult for any message to be received and interpreted in the exact same way as the sender intended.

Even with video-conferencing, the speaker can fashion words, use a specific tone of voice, and shape their face into a supporting expression, but the receiver may still not understand, may be thinking of other things or completely miss the point. Unfortunately, having spoken by video or directly face to face, the speaker then believes that the listener has received the exact same meaning as they intended. That rarely happens.

Putting your story down on 'paper' and asking for a confirmation

After having your distance call, you must follow up with written confirmation of what was discussed and agreed. Include the 'hard stuff' obviously (numbers, timescales, etc.), but don't withhold the softer stuff. 'I feel that . . .'; 'I still have reservations about . . .'

And then you have to ask each person that you have communicated with to return to you the meaning of what was received. If the message doesn't come back the way it was intended, then the sender is able to make adjustments, 'Well that's not quite what I meant, what I meant to say was . . .' Make sure what you are saying is free of jargon.

If you have important messages to send via the written word, make sure you are fully aware of the uphill struggle to deliver meaning – check the document for how easy it is to read. Document software provides readability statistics after you have completed a spell-check. At the bottom of the table that shows the number of words etc., it displays the Flesch Reading Ease test, and the Flesch-Kincaid Grade Level score. The higher the score on the Reading Ease test, the easier the document is to read. Aim for a score of about 70. If it is lower, then shorten the length of sentences and reduce the number of word syllables. The grade level is equivalent to the reading level of students. Aim for a grade of 7–8. If it is much higher, then you may need to simplify the text – really think about *who* you are writing to.

Having built imaginary holograms in the minds of those distant from you, you too will have built an image of them sitting next to you. Displayed photographs reinforce personalities, characters and skill sets. So when you receive new information that will affect them, you instinctively know how they will react. Then you can figure how to deliver the new input to them most effectively.

The challenge of cultural distance

So what's next after an exchange of stories? Culture. It's almost a given that local cultures will differ, sometimes markedly. I have worked in widely varying cultures, all considered Western in origin, and I remember the frustration I felt when I moved employers and found that the previous strong command culture of profit focus had been replaced by an openly democratic style where everyone had a voice and frequently used it. I remember saying to myself, 'Why are you telling me this; I haven't asked for your opinion yet?' I was not used to others expressing themselves so eloquently, and forcibly, that I may have overreacted and shut down conversations too early. I had not adjusted to my new environment, and I did myself a disfavour by culturally distancing myself from my colleagues.

Creating a common culture is incredibly difficult, but it's worth the never-ending effort. A common culture is like glue. It binds everyone together, and as a result, people know how to respond in any circumstance. Decisions get made faster because everyone understands context, backdrop and supported values. A strong identity, coupled with a worthwhile purpose to do good, will encourage pride, and when required, personal sacrifice. The phrase, 'Going the extra mile', while perhaps more management guff, delivers a sense that ordinariness is insufficient to light the path ahead – something more is needed. So let's take a look at some strategies for developing a common bond.

Strategies for 'shortening' cultural distance

In some Asian countries, and in some companies, workers start the day by singing proudly the company song. Sure, some North American companies have led corporate cheerleading sessions (I'm thinking specifically of places like Wal-Mart) but as far as I know, no one in the West has successfully copied the custom of singing the corporate tune because they would be laughed at, and then sentenced to ridicule for eternity and beyond. But the underlying concept is worth examining: getting people to work together in harmony. Unfortunately, forcing everyone to sing each morning fails the doing-good test.

As I have recommended before, diversity is to be prized. You should recruit and benefit from a wide range of ages, upbringing and outlook. Ethnicity, religious beliefs, sexual orientation do not matter. Imagine that members of your family or those working for you are part of a choir – you will need to hear the individual contributions at different times during the music; top tenor, tenor, bass and so forth. When you have problems or challenges, share them, and request input from the most appropriate voice. Having a choir or team comprised only of sopranos will fail to support you when the music or circumstances change.

'We're standing on a burning platform,' Stephen Elop, the then newly appointed Nokia chief executive was quoted widely as saying in 2011. He definitely created a sense of danger and urgency for all employees worldwide. Major changes were afoot, but by using that phrase, Elop tried to convey that everyone was affected equally, a kind of 'we're all in this together' approach. We sink or swim together. Trying to build a common bond. Not dissimilar to the Alamo fortress concept when it's out of time for the cavalry relief; the group are outnumbered by 100 to 1, ammunition is running low, and everyone will need to fight even if injured. That kind of rallying cry might be great for film-makers but, for the everyday leader, it again fails the 'doing good' test. Nokia was soon swallowed up by Microsoft and the company did not recover. Messaging that focuses on the negative in order to motivate is less successful than messaging that focuses on finding a positive solution.

Robert Cialdini, well-known psychologist and expert on the science of persuasion, has often shown that 'injunctive' norms (what ought to be) should follow 'descriptive' norms (what is) in order for purposeful action to follow. Translation, for a city mayor: don't create an ad campaign telling everyone their public parks are dirty because thousands of citizens litter, and then expect people to clean up their local park. Although these claims may be both true and well-intentioned, the ad has missed something critically important: within the message *Many people are doing this* undesirable *thing* lies the powerful and undercutting normative message, *Many people are doing this, so how can* I *make a difference.* Only by aligning descriptive norms (what people typically do) with injunctive norms (what people typically approve or disapprove of) can one optimize the power of normative appeals. Communicators who fail to recognize the distinction between these two types of norms imperil their persuasive effort.[1] A much more powerful message would be: 'I want to thank those citizens who regularly, and without the desire for thanks or recognition, pick up litter discarded by those who care less about our city.'

The case of <u>Hotel Chocolat</u>, binding distant elements through purposive communication

So let's focus on a common-goal strategy that did work and binds many distant elements of a large organization: Hotel Chocolat is a premium UK chocolate brand that has developed and holds to a high standard of ethical behaviour which they have called Engaged Ethics, taking the fair trade movement a step further. The following is not intended to be an advert for the company, but I want to explain how their common culture does good, and that it's the doing-good that sticks everything together – the suppliers, customers and staff.

First, the growers of the cocoa beans. The initiative the company started in Ghana in 2005 to help the local growers was taken to a new level a year later in St Lucia. Then, it appeared that cocoa was on a terminal nosedive across the country with rare old cocoa groves being dug up to plant bananas. The company purchased a beautiful but dishevelled 140-acre estate and nurtured a renaissance of cocoa growing across the picture-postcard Piton-trademarked Island.

Nowadays, they guarantee to buy the whole crop from local growers, creating a sense of confidence in the future; they pay the farmers directly without a middleman's cut; and they offer their own seedlings to local farmers at a discounted price and provide technical help to grow them. At the time of writing in 2019, they have over 213 Island Grower Partners.

Second, the customers. The company has a direct relationship with those who enjoy high-end chocolate. It sells its products online and in its shops. In 1998 it set up The Chocolate Tasting Club, a vast community of chocolate tasters who receive unique selections each month, and whose opinion counts. Hotel Chocolat receives direct feedback from the customer community about all of its activities, good and bad, and adjusts its propositions accordingly. Customers hold the company to account.

Thirdly, the staff. I asked the company's co-founder and chief executive, Angus Thirlwell, 'What do you sell?' Answer: 'Happiness.' To suppliers and to customers. Just imagine climbing out of bed on a cloudy Monday morning to sell 'happiness'. It would make you feel good. No wonder the staff turnover is so low, and the waiting list of potential recruits grows each quarter.

Doing good as a means of binding distant team members together

So, how can you translate what you do into something that 'does good' and brings a team together, no matter how far apart?

As a family unit you could:

- cut their energy or water consumption;
- recruit car-sharing partners;
- recycle more;
- refuse single-use plastic;
- add your own . . .

As a work team you could:

- support a charity;
- engage with local community needs;
- offer advice;
- help local authorities;
- add your own . . .

An organization has to do good for it to have a future. And if it does, then motivation and drive become embedded, because most people want to feel that their job is worthwhile and it matters. Bonus schemes have to be intrinsic, as money is probably the least effective motivator. But a common 'do-good' culture is akin to a virus; a good virus that permeates into every nook and cranny of an organization. People become infected, and by contact with others, pass on the same virus – an epidemic of commitment and contentment derived from doing good.

These are not just loosely based analogies; the social spread of good 'vibes' is actually based on solid research, and, as we saw in Chapter 1, this effect is called 'social contagion'. It turns out your colleague's husband's sister can make you fat, even if you don't know her. A cheerful neighbour has more impact on your happiness than a

Netflix comedy. Harvard professors Nicholas A. Christakis and James H. Fowler[2] found that human social networks exhibit a 'three degrees of influence' property – that is, a tendency for our own personal behaviour to be influenced by people in our proximate social networks. Locally distant interpersonal connections (my wife's colleagues at work, for example) have a high degree of influence with respect to phenomena as diverse as obesity, smoking, cooperation and happiness.

Unfortunately, everyday leaders can't redesign the social networks of their friends and family, and at work they can't log on and purchase a good culture. It has to be developed, nurtured and expanded by genuine 'givers'. It can be used as a tactic for disingenuous management, but it will normally have a short life as the insincerity will become obvious.

Returning to the chocolate theme, the Cadbury and the Rowntree Quaker families demonstrated a pioneering (remember Rolls Royce?) enlightened attitude towards their workers at the beginning of the twentieth century. One hundred and forty-four cottages were built for the Cadbury workers near their factory at Bournville in Birmingham. Infant mortality and death rates in the village in 1915 were half those of Birmingham as a whole. George Cadbury's wife, Elizabeth, played a crucial part in this work. Rowntree founded the village of New Earswick for low-income families in 1902. Education was provided for both children and adults. Rowntree is particularly remembered for his Adult Schools. Cadbury was the first firm to grant its workers a five-day working week and to provide medical facilities, a canteen, leisure activities and community gardens.

I can imagine that both organizations needed fewer managers and less reporting than competing companies that lacked the same level of philanthropy. Both Cadbury's and Rowntree's brands remain today but the Quaker origins that fuelled the ethical behaviour have been lost through changes of ownership.

Customers and workers are attracted to organizations that genuinely do good, but they can be dismissive of those who pay only lip-service to these ideals.

Time to consider your own 'binding' culture

So perhaps it's time to consider your own culture, at home, in your work team, and in your organization. How would you describe it? Choose three adjectives from the list below and try them out with those close to you.

- Money-oriented
- Supportive
- Lonely
- Loving
- Results-driven
- Friendly
- Cynical
- Cost-cutting
- Add your own here:

Do they agree?

Even if you and your colleagues choose the less attractive adjectives, but the team performs well in the upper quartile of its peers, there is no justification for culture change, because whatever you've got, works. But if it performs in the lower quartile then you should consider seeking advice and place culture change on the list of options for recovery.

Let's suppose you are leading a project team across continents. You have a friendly team in New Zealand that works well together; a money-focused team in India, where staff turnover is high; and a new supervisor in Italy who is cutting costs. You can imagine that morale is quite different between these teams. As an everyday leader you start to think about the kind of glue that can bind them together over the longer term, but in the short term, how do you go about stitching them all together in a newly designed patchwork where overall performance is higher?

Here are some things you could try:

1. List those things that are common and bind them together.
2. List those things that separate them.
3. Get the teams' inputs and agreement to the above.
4. Identify the hot-spots of performance and the weak links in the chains.
5. Examine each team's objectives and insert an over-arching one for the whole group.
6. Examine the rewards systems for each team and insert one for the whole group that is heavily weighted.

7. Re-energize the rewards system with a heavily promoted short term (three months or less) objective and a fresh prize for its achievement.
8. Establish a weekly conference call with all team leaders present, to assess progress and obstacles.

Let me know how it goes.

Final Thoughts

Distance is normally measured in miles or time, but it can also be measured in terms of personal connection. One of my wonderful children told me that their old boss never walked the shop-floor, never spoke to staff and never gave them a heads-up on what's happening. He too was leading at a distance, but it was self-imposed. Parents can occasionally, and often unwittingly, lead from a distance when they may be physically at home, but mentally away on the laptop or phone for long periods. Think carefully about being perceived as that kind of everyday leader. Be conscious of who you want them to see, because when you are not there, it's that image that will be the first thing they'll remember.

Question. Decide upon a person or group with whom you feel disconnected – be they next-door neighbours or thousands of miles away, and create some options to improve your understanding of their 'story'.

Name of person or group

The Everyday Leader takes time with individuals, even if they are physically distant, and shows a genuine interest to understand their 'stories'.
The Everyday Leader doesn't just make contact with people when they want something from the other party; they check in regularly ensuring their presence is ever felt even in their absence.

10

Leading integration and alignment

This chapter could easily be two, but I have combined them because although integration and alignment have traditionally been treated as separate issues, they should be combined and tackled together. Indeed, growing research shows that combining the two goals is advantageous on many fronts.[1]

Three 'hypothetical' integration challenges

Imagine that you are called to advise a friend about his forthcoming second marriage and the doubts and fears that person has about bringing two sets of children together under one roof. One set of children are used to fixed meal times and eating together whereas the other set has a more relaxed 'grazing through the day when you're hungry' approach. The two families have different cultures.

Imagine that in an internal re-organization at work, you have been appointed to lead your existing team plus another and then reduce the total headcount by 20 per cent. Your team at work enjoys your trust and works on their own initiative, whereas the team you inherit has been micromanaged for the past three years. The two teams have different cultures.

Imagine that you lead an organization, large or small, and have arranged to merge with another organization, large or small. You know your own organization performs well, whereas the other has experienced difficulties with new product launches and staff retention. The two organizations have different cultures.

How will you integrate disparate groups so that they operate as one team? You have three options:

- *Option 1*: Ask the team you inherit to work your way [how it tends to go].
- *Option 2:* Ask your team to change in order to work as the incoming team has done previously (rare, but a much better option).
- *Option 3*: Attempt a third way, which combines the best of both.

The principles for integration are remarkably similar across all three examples. You've probably made lists before in some fashion, so what are your initial thoughts on integration as the everyday leader? In any order, write them here:

....

....

....

....

....

....

....

Challenge 1: Integrating the family

Let's look first at the advice you will consider offering your friend about bringing the two sets of children together. Unlike the other two work-related challenges you are blind to the nuances of the relationships within the two families and therefore it would be wise to resist offering advice and instead stick to the type of questions that you would ask your friend. She would then have the benefit of being asked to take a step away from the turmoil and the upsets of personal emotions to reflect upon the needs and wants of the individuals involved:

- What does success look like? What are you trying to achieve? Does everyone agree?
- Is the objective one you have defined, constructed, or has it been imposed?
- Has everyone had an opportunity to express their wishes for the future?
- Are you trying to get your way or the best way?
- Are you asking each of the children to conform to a new set of expected behaviours? If so, why?
- Why do you need to do anything at all? Why not let the children develop their own model?

- What are you most concerned about? Why?
- Who are you most concerned about? Why?
- Are there clashes of timetables and logistics? If so, what are the options?
- What are the emotional hangovers from the divorce proceedings? Any current or residual angers?
- What are the visiting rights of the displaced parent[s]?
- How will you split your time? Who is the most needy?
- Are there money pressures? Are there other limitations?
- What about schools, doctors, sports clubs, recreational activities?
- Who will be asked to make to biggest changes? And the smallest?
- What are the activities that could bring them all together to enjoy? What are their shared interests?
- What changes do you think you [your friend] will need to make? And her partner?
- Are you [your friend] prepared to make radical changes to unite the group?

Some of the above questions remain valid for the next two challenges, but before we move on, ask your friend to think about the time it may take before everything settles down into a new family rhythm. Talk to her about the likely disappointments and *volte*-faces, and counsel her to try to maintain the bigger picture in her mind whilst raised voices and even temper tantrums may become commonplace in the short term. Tell her also to watch out for signs of successful integration, however limited, and then to recognize and acknowledge the words or deeds: 'Just thought I'd say "thank you" Claudio or "congratulations" Claudio for . . .'

Challenge 2: Merging two work teams

Next, the internal re-organization at work. Let's re-work some of the above questions into this situation, and add in the requirement for headcount reduction. But this time, the questions are for you:

- Has everyone in both teams been told about the re-organization and the headcount reduction? If not, do it.
- What does success look like? What are you trying to achieve?
- Have you compared the cultures between the two teams? What are the differences?
- Is there a strict timetable? Any flexibility?
- Has everyone had an opportunity to express their wishes for the future?
- Are you trying to get your way or the best way?
- Are you asking each of the team members to conform to a new set of expected behaviours? If so, why?
- Why do you need to do anything at all? Why not let the team members develop their own model for the future?
- How will you determine the roles that will not be needed or are duplicated? Who will you consult? Can you leverage

natural wastage to reduce the headcount or do you need to make people redundant? Can you create or ask for an attractive redundancy package? Will you advertise all the roles for your new enlarged team and ask for applications?

- Can you leverage technology more to create a new work model?
- What are you most concerned about? Why?
- Who are you most concerned about? Why?
- What are the feelings of the individuals about the reorganization? Fears; resentments; anger?
- How quickly can you allay job security concerns?
- How will you split your time? Who is the most needy?
- Apart from headcount are there other limitations?
- Your team has supplier teams and customer teams. Have you spoken with them about the upcoming changes?
- Who will be asked to make the biggest changes? And the smallest?
- What are the activities that could bring them all together to enjoy? What are their shared interests?
- What changes do you think you will need to make to the way that you work?
- Are you prepared to make radical changes to unite the group?

Consider speaking to the team members individually to determine their preferred way of working – some in your team might enjoy more regular contact with you, and some incoming members may have been hoping and praying that they could enjoy more independence.

You may have a majority for a preferred way or you may not, but everyone will have had the opportunity to influence your thinking and they will appreciate it. But if you seek uniformity, ask yourself why. Show the leadership and management style necessary to get the best out of each individual. Lead yourself to be the most flexible of all.

Though you would have preferred to put this off, the 20 per cent reduction has to be completed so that the majority of your staff feel that there isn't a 'winning' or 'losing' original team. Despite the loss of potentially excellent people, this could be an opportune time for you to strengthen the bonds between the two original teams. And that brings us to an often tried, somewhat mocked and rarely successful activity of organized team bonding or team building. These activities can take the form of away-days, often combining light-hearted fun and games with one or two workshops focused on the team's future tasks. If that's your approach, save your money; instead, roll up your sleeves, fix the issues as far as possible, then celebrate and reward the team with an activity which overtly acknowledges and commends the adjustments that everyone will have been trying to make.

I've enjoyed many different corporate cultures during my time in management, from 'head-down, entirely profit focused' to 'let everyone have their say'. I have found it difficult to adjust to the change. I (and, I suspect, you) tend to like it best when it's my (your) way! But I could have performed a lot better in many of my appointments had I been guided by some bedrock everyday leadership principles and a structured approach to integration for newcomers.

Challenge 3: An organizational merger

On a larger scale, either as a small- and medium-sized enterprise (SME) or as a huge multi-national company (MNC), your last challenge involves a merger with another outfit. I don't know of an organization that doesn't have problems with product launches or staff retention post-merger, so that shouldn't bother you too much. Product launches are usually delayed or released with known but fixable faults, and either too many people leave or you don't have enough talent to do the work required in the first place. Too high turnover means there are issues with recruitment, training and/or culture and too few people on deck means you lack the questioning and fresh energy that new recruits bring to the table.

Although the same principles apply as they did with the two previous examples, the scale of integration at an organizational level will present additional challenges. These are my recommendations, based around three stages of the process:

Preparation

Take plenty of time over this point as the outcome dictates your priorities and the pattern of activity. Start by:

- Identifying all of the stakeholders.
- Decide what success will look like to all of the stakeholders – what are you trying to achieve?
- Decide on the 'good' that you will target.
- Start with the knowledge that most mergers and take-overs fail to meet their stated objectives, and final costs and timelines are usually more than double the initial estimates.

- It is essential to get widespread agreement of the culture of both parties, and therefore the acknowledgement that adjustments will be needed by all.
- Delegate all of your usual responsibilities so that you can focus 100 per cent of your time on the mechanics of the merger. Recruit a small project team that represents the interests of both organizations. Bring in an adviser or two from outside who have been through the process before and learned some painful lessons. Re-visit de Bono's 'Six Thinking Hats' model.
- Acknowledge to yourself and to others that merging two organizations is not one of your core competences.
- Understand the reasons for the merger, both publicly stated and hidden; is the link-up pursued from strength or weakness; for growth or survivability; to cut costs or increase opportunities; with a competitor or with an organization in your value chain; to secure new markets or intellectual property
- Know that, the staff of both organizations don't want to merge and will be nervous about what will happen, particularly their own job security; they only identity with their own organization and not the other; they will be cynical about management's ability to complete the task properly; and will be updating their CV and seeking alternative employment. (Can you tell I've been through this before?)
- Know that there will be winners and losers.
- Estimate the costs involved and seek a budget that is five times higher. You might then be able to bring the project in under budget!

- When making changes to systems and processes know that you will introduce four ways of working: the 'old' system; the 'new' system; a bit of both; and a work-around.
- Agree and publicize the process of decision making and dispute resolution, knowing that power struggles will have already started

Implementation

After your prepping and planning work is complete, you now have to act on your vision:

- Agree and communicate the revised vision for the organization.
- Establish senior-level workshops to create a revised strategy for the new enterprise.
- Establish representative workshops for staff to develop the values of the new organization. Bottom-up, not top-down means a better chance of compliance.
- Be prepared to fire those who put themselves first and the organization second. When two managers have both peed on the same tree to mark-out their territory and won't back-down, it will harmful to create a 'winner' and a 'loser'. Get rid of both.
- You will have enormous difficulty trying to combine systems, processes and practices. This may be a wonderful and once-in-a-lifetime opportunity to start with a blank side of A4 and build afresh. (I told you about budget!)
- Create a sense of urgency and issue daily updates to all staff, confronting the brutal truth when necessary. 'We are having difficulty resolving . . . because . . .'

- With all communications, avoid the patronizing public relations speak: 'In putting our customers first . . . blah, blah.' No one believes it and you diminish your own credibility.
- Create a range of timelines for milestones. 'Between November and March we will have concluded . . .' This tactic will remove the possibility that staff will speak to colleagues about missed deadlines.
- When making changes always set up a pilot test or provisional workaround. Don't commit everyone until the unforeseen has been spotted and the risks contained or mitigated.
- Ask all staff for their opinions about the hot-spots: 'What do you believe will be the most difficult thing to resolve?' You will be surprised by how the most mundane issue can raise temperatures among those affected. During a substantial re-location project I led, I was surprised that much of the opposition to the move focused on the lack of a major supermarket near to the new premises. The absence prevented many doing their weekly shop during their lunch-break. I solved that one by contracting for a mid-sized mini-bus to ferry staff to and from the nearest stores every lunchtime.

'Bedding-in'

It's important not to walk away from the changes implemented. You have to follow up to ensure there is understanding, follow-through and compliance:

- Collect difficulties daily from a broad base, but always ask for suggestions of how to overcome them: 'So what are you going to do about it?' Don't let anyone pile problems on your shoulders.
- Set up some early wins and publicize them so that everyone can see progress, even if it's not in their area.
- Reward those same wins, but not necessarily with expenditure. A personal visit from a senior executive to say a simple 'thank you' can prove more powerful.
- Walk and talk, then walk more and talk more. Get out and about to see for yourself. Ask lots of questions, such as: 'What's the biggest problem you have?' 'Tell me about the progress you are making?'
- Try and deal with issues and problems the same day as you receive them. Collecting long lists doesn't work. And remember that there is no right answer. Minor adjustments and work-arounds taken quickly will be needed and then needed again.
- Maintain a visible up-beat and positive demeanour to everyone. Think of yourself as the battery charger for those drained by doubt and uncertainty.

So whether you, the everyday leader, are being asked to integrate children from two disparate families, bring two work teams together, or organize a corporate merger, you can take comfort from the many similarities.

Alignment 101

Although *integration* can be a substantial challenge to the everyday leader, it is easy when compared to organizing or reorganizing *the alignment* of all the disparate teams towards the same familial or corporate goals. So when you are integrating two teams, you need to be mindful of the need to align their work with other teams in the organization in order to avoid duplication, over and under-laps and to ensure that the work contributes to the overall goals and objectives of the organization. Alignment means that every individual, every team and every department uses the exact same yardstick or reference as the back-drop to their decision-making. 'Does what we are about to do, accelerate our progress towards the achievement of the organization's objectives?' If it doesn't then it shouldn't be approved.

During the first phase of integrating the two sets of children, it may be commonplace for one set to be pulling in a different direction than the other. Naturally, each wants it their way, and you may have to give them space. But with your leadership they should gradually come together and recognize a new norm. The tipping point for alignment comes when decisions by each of the group members are taken unselfishly so as to benefit the whole family. It's akin to what happens on a construction project. Imagine building a new house: the plumbers, electricians and tilers complete their own specific jobs in the bathrooms, each knowing that they have to co-ordinate each stage of their work with their colleagues. But when problems arise, they must co-operate with each other to ensure that the homeowner gets what she wanted. They have to be flexible and adaptable, adjusting what they do and when they do it so as to achieve the desired outcome. They and their work has to be lined up.

I like to think of alignment in a fairly literal sense and imagine cycle racing teams in the Tour de France. Individual teams, such as Sky, now renamed as Team Ineos™, compete each leg in tandem, eight cyclists race one behind the other. Their goal is to bring their leader to the front at a specific moment and seven of the team are sacrificed, one after the other, in the process. If, during a stage, the leader suffers a puncture or a mechanical failure and has to drop back to the team's service vehicle, then three or four of the team fall back with him. After the leader's bike is repaired or replaced, the team protects the lead cyclist and paces him back into the main peloton. Each cyclist has a specific role yes, but every decision they make during the stage is made in the context of how it might affect the team and its leader. There are plenty of individual roles, but each is subordinate to the shared responsibility for overall success.

In a family, similar alignment principles apply. One child could be responsible for clearing the meal table and loading the dishwasher as part of an over-arching objective of having a clean and tidy home. So, knowing that overall objective means that each family member would readily accept their undefined responsibility to pick up litter or mop a spillage. Doing something out-of-role for the common good.

In a commercial organization there are departments such as sales, marketing, manufacturing, operations, IT, HR, finance, etc. The idea that they are all aligned towards achieving a common goal is highly unlikely and to many inside the organization, may even seem absurd. The organization can only perform as well as the weakest link; each function can only perform as well as the weakest team, and each team can only perform as well as the weakest person. That means the organization is aligned for weakness. Everyone is trying to compensate for weaknesses; a manufacturing problem limits output so sales and marketing adjust; an IT issue limits invoice data gathering and therefore revenue in the period. In most organizations, supply chain planning is a cross-functional effort, but sales, marketing, finance and operations traditionally specialize in portions of the planning activities, which can result in conflicts over expectations, preferences and priorities.

Because there are weaknesses, projects are created to address them. Each function has their own discrete projects, as well as contributing to those that are cross-functional. Each department wants budget to improve performance. Department heads battle for more money and political in-fighting is common.

How to build alignment?

I have heard the phrase 'we are a sales-led, market-driven organization' many times and I question its validity. To me a seamless approach that cuts across functions would be more successful. I also question the use of the word 'division' in an organization. The word literally means separating something into parts or more negatively, disagreement between two or more groups, typically producing tension or hostility. To me 'multiplier' would be better – it tells everyone that their job is to add value to what the other functions are doing.

So how to build alignment or reinforce it? Look to these seven areas for help:

1 *Strategies.* Re-visit the corporate strategies, reinforce and magnify their importance and relevance to all decision-making. Try to paint them in human terms by using real people as exemplars. People can empathize with other people, but not with so-called 'management speak'. For example, for Hotel Chocolat, it meant that their 'ethical engagement' goal translated to helping one individually named farmer. Photographs of him, his family, his farm, his income and outgoings, enabled decision-makers in the UK to understand the impact they had on his circumstances. And by helping him they helped all the farmers. Ethical engagement delivered.

2 *Projects.* List all of the projects in progress. Compare and contrast objectives. Do the employee goals line up with team goals, the team goals with departmental goals, and the departmental goals with the enterprise goals? Ask yourself if everyone is pulling in the same direction. If not, then modify or cancel those that don't. Speak with the project team leaders individually and ask them to recognize the 'bigger picture' and the obligation they have to contribute towards it. If that does not work, and there is resistance from some, consider replacing those that do not inspire your confidence.

3 *Culture.* Ask yourself whether you have the right culture to succeed in your endeavours. Is the organization focused on doing good? Do the senior heads co-operate with one another or compete? Either way their behaviour will be replicated further down the organization. Have one or two heads been in post for more than four years and as a result has their department

become their fiefdom? Maybe it's time to swap them around and give them different teams and different responsibilities.

4 *People.* Design and deliver small workshops to every team in the organization to identify the 'hot spots' of disconnect and non-alignment. Seek their work-around options, and commission the corrective actions. Make budget available.

5 *Systems.* Does the output of one system feed the input requirements of the next, or does the data need to be re-entered? Duplication of effort is hugely demotivating to all involved.

6 *Rewards.* Where appraisal systems and/or bonus schemes involve personal objectives, ensure that the goals for the entire enterprise are included. I've never been a fan of individual bonus schemes because targets can never be set fairly, and success cannot be secured without the involvement, co-operation and contribution of others. But a profit sharing scheme, such as the one operated by John Lewis in the UK and many others around the globe, keeps the decision-making relevant to the goals of the organization.

7 *Look outside.* Using external facilitators can prove rewarding when trying to improve the alignment of an organization as individuals are more likely to open up about the real issues than they would to other employees of the same enterprise.

Question. Think of a couple of groups that could be better aligned and then imagine yourself as the consultant chosen to improve the situation. What are your options?

Name of Group 1	**Name of group 2**

The Everyday Leader searches for disconnects between people, teams, processes and systems raises awareness of them, and then rolls up their sleeves and corrects them.
The Everyday Leader doesn't assume that improvements cannot be made and that the way it is, is the way it should remain. If a team is not aligned, people are listened to, and a solution is sought.

11

Leading self-motivation

This chapter deals with your role in helping others to lead themselves more effectively and to be far less dependent on you as an everyday leader. Without a reasonable level of autonomy and self-motivation, your friends, family members and colleagues will always need you to make their decisions for them; instruct them to complete every step, and steal the time you need to devote on other high-level tasks or indeed the time required to help yourself.

Avoiding the temptation of doing it all yourself

We all know why it's so hard at times to let go and allow others to take on a role. It's because, in the short run at least, it's far quicker and easier for *you* to do something that you already know how to do well, rather than ask someone else with less experience or apparent ability to step in and do it for you. Likewise, you often step in and do things for others because again, in that immediate cost–benefit calculation made quickly in your head, waiting for someone with inferior skills to finish a task is way more time-consuming than you doing it for them. And if you did allow them to work it out for themselves, did you still have a thought bubble with the words 'it would have been quicker to do it myself' pop up beside you?

Similar situations abound in which your desire for control makes it impossible for others to develop their own self-motivation. However aspirational it might be for you, as a parent, to tell your teenage son or daughter to 'Make sure you're home by 11pm', it's still perceived as an order. Saying to one of your workers 'Make sure I have that report on my desk by Friday' is also not motivational. Both are usually resented by the receiver as they had their own plans which may (or may not) have coincided with yours.

'Why 11pm?' is heard by the parent. The manager hears the same 'Why?' but transformed into the more politically acceptable format of 'I'm visiting another site on Thursday ... will Monday be OK?' This second phrasing is still asking the same question, 'Why Friday?'

Talking with a group of friends the other day, I asked about the situation of a mutual friend's oldest son. He is 35 now. The response: 'Harry has no drive or ambition. He's happy and perfectly content in a rather mundane job, even though his Ivy-League University degree would predict a far more senior and responsible job. But he'll never change.'

Lack of self-motivation can prove very frustrating for those living or working close by. So let's try to help Harry develop a bit more self-motivation and in doing so, offer guidance to those parents, little league and junior coaches, managers, and executives who are seeing those close to them failing to reach their true potential, however happy they may appear on the outside.

How to do this? It starts with the everyday leader realizing that their job is not to step in and 'fix every problem', but to create the environment in which others can develop and flourish; to try things that they are not immediately great at doing; to allow others to fail but each time allowing them try again in order to improve; and gradually encouraging them to take on more and more responsibility.

I know this is a huge generalization, but most leaders take on way too many tasks and assume far too much responsibility. This is a crucial point, because developing your leadership role involves *doing* less, but *thinking* more.

What is self-motivation?

First, let's be clear what we are talking about. Self-motivation is an ability built up from the inside, a force that allows you to do something without being directed, influenced or persuaded by someone else. Self-motivated people have the drive and determination to set themselves a goal; overcome obstacles; use setbacks to re-invigorate and re-energize; and to deploy their dedication and commitment to overcome a challenge. Entrepreneurs are usually considered to be self-motivated but everyday examples of self-motivation, which you may have overlooked because they seem so mundane, are ever-present:

- Getting up in the morning at a time of your choosing to go for a run.
- Checking fluid levels and the tire pressure on your car regularly without prompting.

- Completing household tasks and small repairs before anyone asks you.
- Starting a business plan.
- Voluntarily giving up smoking, exercising more or eating healthier food.
- De-cluttering the garage or house.

The list could go on, but by now you get the picture. All of us have completed at least one of those tasks, which means we are all capable of being self-motivated. When people are self-motivated they are often seeking satisfaction from within. This is the *intrinsic* motivator. Sometime it helps if there is a reward or an acknowledgement, which is an *extrinsic* reason. Which of the two is motivating you depends on the situation.

For example, I decided last year to learn to drive an articulated large goods vehicle (LGV). No-one asked me to do it and I didn't need to do it, but I felt I would enjoy the process and the challenge of learning the theory and the regulations for driving a 44-ton, 54ft-long vehicle through the narrow streets of Britain. Risk was involved, as I could have scraped the side of the vehicle or not passed the government's official driving test, and how would that have made me feel? But if successful, I would have felt immense pride and my reward would therefore have been an intrinsic one. Now let's imagine I'd been let go of my job at the local assembly plant and with a young family I need to find a job. Reading in the paper of the desperate shortage of LGV truck drivers in Britain I enrolled in the driving school to boost my chances of finding a job quickly. I passed the test and found a job within a month of completing the driving course. Because I needed to learn how to drive a large truck for money, the reward was an extrinsic one. In both cases, though, I was not following orders or waiting for direction; I was self-motivated to complete the course.

Why you need to foster self-motivation in those you lead

The other question to ask, is why? That is, why is it so important to foster self-motivation in others? There are many reasons but one principle stands above all others. In economics it's known as the principle of 'comparative advantage', developed many years ago by nineteenth-century economist David Ricardo to explain why countries trade with each other.

The explanation before Ricardo seemed rather simple. I trade with another country because I lack what the other has and vice versa. Prior to British industrial decline and global warming, the archetypal example was always Portugal selling wine to Britain, and Britain (which was far too cold and damp to make wine) selling clothes and textiles back to Portugal. This seems rather obvious. The counterintuitive and remarkable feature of Ricardo's theory, however, was that even if a country like Britain was better and more productive at producing everything than Portugal (including wine), it would still benefit itself (and its trading partner) by concentrating on what it was *best adapted to* and *relatively most productive* at producing, and allowing its trading partners to produce the rest. Each country would benefit in this example by maximizing their total output, lowering their total costs, and thereby engaging in trade.

As a leader you may have the *absolute advantage* over your family members, colleagues or employees (i.e. the requisite skills and experience to do most of what you ask of others, and to do it better, faster and quicker) but in relative terms, you are not the best at everything. You have a *relative advantage* in that you are great at some things and only really good at all the others. As a leader, you add more value by focusing on what you're great at, and jettisoning the rest. With time, and no longer doing all the day-to-day tasks that you were really good at, you will find that your team, family members and work colleagues, providing they are self-motivated, will fill the void that you have left behind.[1]

How does one foster self-motivation in those who seem to lack it?

So now that we have pinned down more concretely what self-motivation is and why it's important to develop in others, we are left with an obvious question: how to do it? Maybe if we return to the example of my friend's son, Harry, we can begin to explore some techniques and strategies.

To help Harry become self-motivated requires that a goal be set that has some risk attached. Easier said than done, as not setting goals is the problem with those lacking self-motivation. Forget risk for the moment; our options are extremely limited as the primary quality of self-motivation is that the goal isn't triggered or encouraged by outside agents. Harry has to do this himself, so direct phrasing like 'have you thought about?', or 'why don't you?' are not viable options.

Indirectly planting a seed by setting up scenarios and opportunities for Harry to 'discover' his goal has to be the only way. Encouragement tactics of an indirect nature that steer someone *towards* a goal might include:

- identifying a subject or issue he is interested in or spoken about and offering up chances to learn more about them;
- leaving a self-help book in plain sight;
- giving a biography, book or film, of someone Harry admires, as a present;
- inviting him to meet, for a coffee or lunch, someone who is self-motivated, and who has the same or similar interest;
- set an example for them by describing something you've 'decided to do . . .'
- don't be afraid to ask questions like 'How do you think it would make you feel if you tried . . .'

Now that you understand the principle at work and have seen a few examples, think of the 'Harry' in your life (i.e. friend, work colleague, spouse or sibling lacking self-motivation) and add your own encouragement tactics here:

....

....

....

....

....

And we mustn't forget that negative scenario planning – i.e., discouragement tactics – can also work to steer someone *away* from a path that is suboptimal for them:

- 'Do you really plan on being in the same organization when you retire?'
- 'When did you last re-decorate this room?' (knowing the answer is never)
- 'I see that Omar has a new car, how old is yours now?'
- 'Is that a new shirt you're wearing?' (knowing that it isn't)
- 'Do you think you'll ever go see that . . .'
- 'How would it make you feel if you never once . . .'

Again you can add your own thoughts below:

....

....

....

....

....

Be patient; keep trying the above. If unsuccessful, you will have to partner with Harry and suggest something that you could do together, such as: 'Why don't we . . . [enter the local fun run together or climb Mount Everest].'

Keep it simple (the Everest suggestion can be mentioned playfully) and choose something you're sure he likes, but ask Harry to organize it. Check the progress he makes regularly and congratulate him on his efforts. Complete the task and choose the next. Repeat until you ask him to suggest your next partnership activity: 'OK, now I've suggested the previous two things we've done together, why don't you choose next?' I bet Harry has often wanted to do some interesting things but lack of self-motivation (and lack of practice at choosing and organizing) has meant that he's done nothing about it. You're attempting to change 'wanting to do' into 'planning to do' and 'doing'.

Sometimes not so subtle encouragement is warranted: 'Can you organize it Harry, as I'm saturated with work issues at the moment?' Progress will occur, but in small steps.

Next up, tackling risk. Most of us are risk averse. And yet confronting our fears and dealing with them, can lead to an improvement in our self-esteem. It turns out that experiencing fear in a safe, controlled environment can be euphoric. Have a think about Harry's level of unacceptable risk. Is it more about potential danger to the body or to feelings? Is Harry afraid of being thought a 'failure'? Has Harry allowed his history of not succeeding in something dear to him, to quieten his ambition? Is he saying to himself, 'I have failed before and didn't like the feeling; therefore I won't put myself into the same position again'? This needs testing.

Finding the real reason(s) for lack of motivation and planting the right mental seed(s)

If you are not making the progress you had expected, then perhaps it's time for you to face him directly: 'Harry, I feel I have to say this to you – I feel that you have the talent and ability to achieve higher level goals, and yet to me, you seem to have lost your mojo. You seem to settle for less these days. Has something happened?'

Just as something may have happened to Harry to blunt his self-motivation, you could also plant a few different seeds in his mind that may well develop into a catalyst for change, from 'wanting to do' to 'doing'.

For example, I was a smoker for over 20 years, and six months before my landmark 40th birthday I started to contrast my smoking habit against my fondest wish to see my children grow, marry and start their own families. I saw smoking as a threat to my longevity, and decided to stop. I didn't find it too difficult and for over 30 years later I haven't touched a single cigarette.

Looking back now, I find it interesting how this change came about. I had thought many times before my 40th that it would be advisable to quit, but I didn't change my behaviour. It turns out I needed a *real* reason. The thought of missing out on future family moments was it. The lesson: if you're looking at someone currently lacking self-motivation, think of the kind of mental seeds you could plant in their minds? Many will fail, but maybe one or two may take root and start to grow.

Danny, a talented multi-skilled tradesman, visited our house today to fix another fault with our newish home. In the four months that we haven't seen him, he has lost nearly 30lbs in weight. I asked him why and he gave me a generic answer about wanting to be fit. But having worked on the self-motivation chapter that morning, I pressed him to describe the actual moment he said to himself, 'It's time I lost weight.' He paused and then said, 'I have a young child, my first, and when she cries, I found running upstairs exhausting, having to pause to draw breath before attending to her. I decided I didn't want to be one of those parents that couldn't play with their children.' The seed was planted with his daughter's birth, the catalyst emerged when her cries demanded his energy and focus.

It's time to think of the possible catalysts for Harry.

Self-guidance and self-talk as tools for finding your motivation to change

In Chapter 1 we discussed the interplay between two contrasting inner voices, 'shall I stop to help Joe, or carry on driving to my appointment.' It's possible that Harry's inner voice is sometimes telling him that, 'I'm no good at ...' And every time he hears this demotivating inner voice it becomes more powerful and more difficult to challenge. Perhaps you know someone who talks themselves down?

Contrast the development of a more positive inner voice. There is a large body of research with roots in psychology, but stretching over into fields as diverse as sports medicine and management coaching, which demonstrates the power of our minds to rewire themselves through proactive and repetitive training. The most popular examples come from high-performance athletics, where at one time the only coaching was physical and almost all of it focused on improving endurance, flexibility or strength and mastering technical aspects of the sport in question. The missing factor, of course, was the mental component, until a group of sports psychologists realized that 'rehearsing' a routine, as one might do in figure skating, clearly and deliberately in your brain could improve the performance by a clear margin over competitors who didn't.[2]

Numerous studies in management have equally shown that purposive thoughts, rehearsed and repeated (sometimes aloud), can help people complete tasks by stated deadlines, and achieve higher overall levels of workplace performance.

What's curious is that the act of rehearsing and verbalizing one's intended goals makes a noticeable difference. In other words, it's not enough to loosely entertain an idea or to think about what you intend to do, you have to really imagine doing it and focus hard on how you would do it (i.e. articulating all the steps needed). Adding a verbal commitment, even if it is only articulated to yourself, can further improve your likelihood of successfully following through on your goal.

This kind of self-talk might seem strange (indeed how is it that we can fool ourselves into doing something?) but it has been shown to work.

Embracing failure and instilling resilience

Resilience is another quality and characteristic of a self-motivated person. You know that when asked to do a simple job around the house, usually two things happen: firstly, this simple job is much more complicated than you imagined and will need the precise same tool that you loaned to a friend or neighbour who hasn't returned it; secondly, it will take between two or three times longer than you predicted. At which point, you become increasingly annoyed and frustrated, until you tell yourself to calm down, slow down, and postpone the activity that, by now, you had thought you'd be enjoying instead.

Knockbacks and failures make some people give up ('I can't do it sweetheart, I'll get someone in to do it next week, OK?'), whereas for others it makes them re-double their efforts, accepting disappointments as an infusion of energy ('I'm just going to town to get the right tools and equipment, I should be about an hour'. 'Don't bother darling, sorry I asked, leave it for another day, you'll miss the match on television.' 'Darling, I've started and I'm going to finish.') Which is your most favoured response?

So, can you teach resilience? I believe the quality can be improved by immersing the target into those worlds where stamina is one of the most important attributes. I'm not suggesting that Harry takes up marathon swimming or running, but I am suggesting that perhaps he can be introduced to those individuals and teams where mental toughness is a prime requirement. Learning by observing and taking it in through a process of social osmosis.

Beware of the self-motivation destroyers

Yes, self-motivation is extremely difficult for the everyday leader to impart on others, but it's well worth the time and effort. However, what is less appreciated is that self-motivation is extremely easy to kill.

Take the case of my grandson, William, who worked happily in a coffee shop in the centre of Cambridge for over a year before starting university. He started by washing the pots and plates before waiting at tables and serving the customers. Then one day, rather suddenly, he resigned. It turned out it was because of the behaviour of a new manager. When the coffee shop got busy, the manager ordered Will to wait on tables. Several times Will, when waiting on tables, noticed that the stack of unwashed plates and pots were becoming a severe limitation on future service, so he swapped duties without being told and started to wash the pots. Once the new manager spotted this, he felt his directive had been transgressed and said, 'I told you to wait at tables when we're this busy, Will. Now get out there!' Will tried to explain the logic behind his initiative but to no avail. After several occurrences, Will became robbed of his self-motivation and initiative. Unhappy, he resigned.

Will's experience of working in the shop over the previous twelve months and coping successfully with very busy periods meant nothing to the new manager. Like so many others who quit, it was the ill-informed and poorly trained manager William left, not the company or job, which he enjoyed.

Will's manager didn't give himself enough time to identify those people that require little or no supervision – knowing they had the self-motivation (and experience) to do what was needed – and those that require more management direction. The decisions Will's manager took heaped more and more responsibility for decision making upon himself. Without self-motivation, orders and instructions become more commonplace, and gradually more detailed.

Orders are an exercise in authority. But there is always a price to pay, with each directive a slight diminishment of the receivers' self-motivation. Played over the longer term, the receivers of these orders stop taking the initiative; stop looking for problems and opportunities and instead wait for the authority figure to order the specific sequence of their actions. That means the authority figure has to increase their level of intervention to get things done, stealing the time they have for other more important work. The longer it goes on, the more time is stolen. At work, the manager gets frustrated with the employee and credits the person with a below-average rating in their annual appraisal. A downward spiral of performance and culture ensues.

Using what we've read in this chapter, let's look at alternatives, starting with our opening examples.

Your teenage son is about to head out on a Friday night and instead of saying, 'Make sure you're home by 11pm', you stop for a millisecond and think about his self-motivation before saying, 'What time will you be home tonight, because I'm going to lock up and go to bed at 11.30pm?' Your son's response might well be, 'Well in that case, I'll stay overnight at Josh's parents' house. The movie ends rather late.'

Or how about your employee and the state of the report? If you try a similar new tactic, 'When will you have that report completed, as I have a meeting scheduled to discuss it with the Union on Tuesday?' You might get the following response, 'Well in that case, I'll get it done by close of play Friday, so you have the weekend to read it.'

Providing a reason for your request (e.g. I need to know when you're coming home because I plan on going to bed early) and implying a consequence (e.g. if I don't have that report on my desk by Friday, I won't be able to read it in time for my meeting with the Union) will help embed it in the receiver's mind and helps them manage their time and activity.

While these may not be the ideal questions masquerading as requests, it does leave the receiver with a sense of responsibility and some measure of autonomy. Having answered a question and made a verbal promise, the receiver carries a self-imposed duty to deliver.

And, most importantly, a feeling that *they* have made the decision, not the authority figure.

Having made a verbal commitment, a receiver is less likely to renege, meaning that you won't have to wait up until nearly midnight, nor will you have to chase down the report.

The next day, you might want to say 'thank you' to your offspring, or to your colleague at work for delivering on their promise. If that's the case, stop yourself. It may seem counterintuitive but remember what this chapter is about: self-motivation. Refrain from thanking them because it creates the impression that they did what they did only for you.

Instead use a word like 'congratulations' or 'well done', which is much better. Why? Because you set up the question so that they made their own decision about what they would do. Discouraging dependency and encouraging independence and self-motivation is the role of the everyday leader.

Final thoughts

When trying to help Harry in his home and social environment, you have enjoyed the time and opportunity to undertake a few experiments, but supposing Harry is one of your team members at work. There you do not have the same luxury. So what are your options?

Identify three examples of when and/or where Harry's lack of self-motivation has caused you to become more involved in the situation than you should have, and then call him on it, but do so in private. 'Harry, we need to have a chat about what I perceive as a slight deterioration in your pro-activity and your problem solving. I am raising the issue with you informally as I want to understand if there is anything happening at work or outside work that is affecting your normal drive and enthusiasm?'

I already know that you are self-motivated because you are reading this book. You wouldn't have bought it otherwise. You have decided that you are in charge of your own actions, not someone else. But how self-motivated are the people around you? If you have a Harry at work and see the potential in him, then you may wish to consider mentoring him personally, asking someone else to mentor him, or providing him with a career coach or work counsellor. You could be Harry's 'Tiger Mom'.

If, on the other hand, you don't think Harry has the potential to perform a lot better, then maybe it's time for you to think about upgrading your team and giving Harry the opportunity to find something he may enjoy more. Both situations are tough and require delicate wording, but in either case, I wish you best of luck.

Question. Select a named individual who you believe lacks self-motivation and create a few subtle (and not so subtle) tactics to try to change their outlook and become more goal-oriented.

Name of individual	**Encouragement tactics**

The Everyday Leader supports and reinforces the self-motivation of others so as to increase their own ability to concentrate on bigger picture stuff.
The Everyday Leader doesn't use their power and authority to diminish the self-image nor blunt the self-motivation of those around them.

12

Leading empowerment

This chapter focuses on the practice of 'empowerment', once a fashionable management-speak word meaning, 'giving somebody the strength, confidence and scope to act on their own initiative'. But empowerment is no passing fad, it is actually one of the most enduring and meaningful managerial practices and one that has been linked with positive outcomes for firms and workers alike. Every parent will understand that, for them, empowerment means giving their children roots to grow and wings to fly.

Establishing the parameters of empowerment

Strength comes from a secure and stable platform. When throwing a ball for your dog, you plant your feet, one behind the other, as a balanced platform for the throwing action. When mobile cranes arrive at a construction site, the driver lowers the legs to the ground, creating the platform for lift. As a parent you provide a safe and secure environment as your children's platform before they begin to test their own capabilities. Planting roots.

Confidence is built through trial and error, gaining experience of different levels of risk, both physical and emotional; of accomplishment and disappointment; of success and failure. And you must know failure in order to appreciate success.

Scope establishes the parameters upon which your children or co-workers can exercise their autonomy and decision-making skills. Beyond a certain scope they will know to come to you and ask for advice or permission.

At home, as the children grow, successful parents gradually give their offspring more and more responsibility and the freedom to make their own decisions. They delegate.

Empowerment, though, is not always easy for the everyday leader to figure out. Test your knowledge: are these empowering statements?

- 'From next Monday you are responsible for making your own bed and tidying the bedroom.'
- 'Starting Saturday I want you to lay the table for mealtimes.'

No, these are not empowering statements; they provide some scope and autonomy but they are instructions. I can make someone responsible and accountable, but it's not empowerment. But statements like these: 'Why don't you pack your own bag for a sleepover with Antonio' and, 'If you ever want to make some cakes, you know where everything is' are empowering. Providing that the parent resists the temptation to check that the travel bag contains a toothbrush, and noticing that the heat was set way too high, lets the cakes burn to a crisp. Allowing them to learn.

When building empowerment, consequences are important and lessons learned are ideally discussed immediately afterwards, building confidence. This means children will learn to trust themselves and their decisions. And next time packing the toothbrush, and researching the correct oven temperature. Providing them with wings.

You can grant authority to pack an overnight bag or bake cakes, but also establish limits. 'Mum, while you were out I made myself an omelette,' shows initiative and confidence. Good job. Your child felt empowered.

But what about, 'Mum, I've invited 15 of my school chums around later for a party.' Your child felt empowered. Good job. How would you react? 'Sorry sweetheart, another time perhaps as we have some of our friends round tonight, tomorrow is good though.' Or 'No way José, I don't want people throwing up on the new carpet. Next time you want a party, ask.'

Some parents would say that organizing a party without prior approval would be overstepping the mark. But marks are more like lines in the sand than a border wall, difficult to pre-judge and settings vary between parents. I would say that, only by overstepping them, would anyone know where the mark was in the first place. Acting with too much caution by either parent or child can be self-limiting. Risks have to be taken and ideally recognized and mitigated, but removing them completely may severely limit learning and potential. Establishing the right scope of autonomous decision making is often more 'art' than 'science.'

Empowerment: what it is, what it isn't and what it does to your kids

I've heard a lot about helicopter parents and snowflakes. Both terms apply just as much at work as they do at home and I'll come to that later. But back at home, a helicopter parent is over-protective, hovering and fussing over their child, monitoring their every move, swooping in whenever they think something may not be quite right. The parent's obsessive desire for the child's success and safety may, inadvertently and unintentionally, cause the child more harm than good. Children of over-protective parents tend to be under-confident and withdrawn. While parental involvement is related to many positive child outcomes, if not developmentally appropriate and veering towards the 'helicopter style', it is associated with higher levels of child anxiety and depression, later in life, and there is a growing body of psychological research to back this up.[1] Empowering, it is not.

And are 'helicoptered' children more likely to become snowflakes? Research has shown that helicopter parenting is associated with low self-efficacy, alienation from peers, and a lack of trust;[2] in a word, helicoptering is associated with more 'delicate' personas.

I personally love the term 'snowflake', perfectly formed but insubstantial and liable to dissolve in front of you. A term first coined in the 1990s, a snowflake is someone who believes that they are unique and special. Who doesn't? But snowflakes are more – they are easily offended, intolerant, and find it difficult to handle opposing views to their own. They complain quickly and seek safe spaces in which to retreat from the harsh realities of everyday life. Some believe they are anti-free-speech because they shout down those that think differently. And there's a generation of them apparently.

But do they have the strength and confidence to act on their own initiative? I think they do in a confined and sympathetic environment, but they may find it more difficult when you add generational and cultural variances into the mix. The bottom line is that we shouldn't forget that snowflake behaviour (i.e. heightened sensitivity and a sense of overblown entitlement) is not necessarily written into our genes; malformed feelings can be fomented just as they can be downplayed by intelligent managerial and parenting techniques.[3]

Selfish empowerment turns into social change

Women feel empowered today more than ever. Strong, assertive, and claiming their rights to be treated as equals at home, in the community and at work. Moreover, women have not been empowered by men, they have empowered themselves and been very successful in many cultures. The heroic efforts of the suffragettes in the Western world, and the role that women played on home soils during major wars, laid the platform for today's equal rights movement. They shook up the system and demanded change. Our societies are better for it.

But what separates an empowering movement from a selfish claim for more?

I asked myself this question while writing this chapter, i.e. whether empowerment enjoys some kind of parallel with selfishness? And I believe it does, in the best way possible. Giving somebody the strength and confidence to act on their own initiative may indeed lead to selfish actions, but empowerment contains the potential for a wider application than the purely singular. Emmeline Pankhurst – a leading suffragette founded the Women's Social and Political Union in 1903, which used militant tactics to agitate for women's suffrage. She died in 1928, shortly before women were given full voting rights in Britain. She didn't just act for herself a hundred or so years ago, but rather for all women, as did Malala Yousafzai, who was shot in the head by the

Taliban when she campaigned for girl's rights to education in Pakistan. These two brave women felt injustice on a personal level, and took power into their own hands to correct it. They were joined by others who were equally brave.

Empowering your home

Earlier, I mentioned that most parents set boundaries, empowering their children up to a loosely defined point or scope of action, which they move gradually further out as the children grow and develop into young adults. But Emmeline and Malala were incensed and outraged by the 'point' set for them, and courageously marched over it with their sisters, placards waving for the newspaper photographers of the nineteenth century and social media of the twenty-first.

Vicki Psarias is a modern-day mum with two children, a prolific blogger and vlogger, and a champion of women's rights. Her digital 'magazine of my life' energizes and touches millions around the world, with quantifiable success.[4] I spoke with Vicki, and learned that her determination to empower other women to take a greater control over their lives, to inspire them, and to instil a higher level of self-confidence, consumes her waking hours. She is passionate, articulate and dedicated to her cause. Vicki, and others like her, are proud and honest mums, and though they are not protesting on the streets, they are mobilizing millions and they are the Pankhurst's of our digital age.

So how empowered do you feel? Ready to shake the house? Ready to shake your local community; your church, golf club, or craft society? What about at work? I'm not asking whether you would actually shake, I'm asking whether you feel empowered to shake? Do you feel strong enough and confident enough to take power or do you need empowerment to be granted to you? After thinking about yourself, look around at those close to you. Would you describe them as leading a potential vanguard movement against injustice or for a better tomorrow, or are they in the van following?

As an everyday leader at home, you will teach your children to take the initiative and act for themselves and for the benefit of the entire household and the common good. If you could tap into their inner voices, you might hear them say quietly to themselves, 'I can see that unless I load the dishwasher to clean the plates and saucepans, dinner will be delayed and the food cold.' I bet you undertake to do the equivalent in your communities, and for your friends and colleagues.

Empowering your workplace

Empowered up to a point is important at work too. In business, and not-for-profit organizations, employees are empowered up to a point, be it a financial one or a cultural one. Any empowerment must set the boundaries. In organizations empowerment has been something of a fashion for the past couple of decades. It's often quoted in company material, both internal and external, and yet there has been a consistent disconnect between what executives believe they have done, and what those that are supposed to be empowered, actually feel is the reality. Executives have led policy but not led people or their emotions.

In one of my previous corporate incarnations, I told my staff of over a hundred customer service agents that they could escalate a problem to the main board director without going through different management layers, including me – they could and should go straight to the top and call for rapid action when it was needed. I told them face-to-face and in written communications. Repeatedly. I sat back and waited for the director to call me saying: 'Why John, am I getting all these calls from your people. What's going on?' In two years I didn't get one!

I often asked myself and them, why? And I worked out that they didn't feel it was right. They preferred to act the way they always had, escalating through evermore senior management positions, even though that delayed a resolution for the customers. It was a cultural issue, and no amount of urging by me or my colleagues in other teams would have much of an effect.

If you have worked in a culture where empowerment bows to a more rigid discipline, suddenly introducing it will have limited success. This was found to be one of the limiting factors in a meta-analysis of empowerment research titled 'When empowering employees works, and when it doesn't', published in the *Harvard Business Review*. The authors found that empowerment is easy to say but hard work and time-consuming to enact. It is easier for a new business or a small company, but a major challenge for larger organizations. And of course, it is culturally sensitive. Some national cultures will find it easier than others.[5]

Factors that work in empowering your employees

We looked at organizational culture in Chapter 8, so what are the recommendations for a successful roll-out of an adjusted culture, one where everyone feels more empowered than previously? Here they are:

1 *Start at the top of the entire organization.* The main person, the CEO, has to lead by example. Not only do they have to encapsulate their vision of how life will be after the changes, they have to provide reasons for the changes, and where the positive impact will be felt. The CEO has to communicate it, reinforce it with repetition during multi-media presentations, but also give examples of what they have already adjusted to doing personally. Which of their powers have they entrusted to their lieutenants at the top of the organization? And to what level? The CEO has to state the benefits to him or herself and to those he or she has empowered, and they have to be real benefits. Photos and quotes from those who have been newly empowered should be included.

2 *Clearly targeted.* What is the goal? Which group or groups will feel the benefit? It is usually done to improve customer satisfaction levels; to improve response times; to handle complaints faster; to deal with compensation claims more efficiently. But also think about the positive effect on other groups such as suppliers. Some organizations treat suppliers appallingly while others are more co-operative. Don't forget the media and the reputation of the organization. You may be able to identify several targets for this initiative.

3 *Trust.* This is a crucial element as it goes to the heart of empowerment. And the question you have to ask yourself at the start of the culture change is, 'Do I trust the people who I am about to empower with more authority, sign-off powers and money?' Can you instantly answer 'yes' because you have

staff who are mature, level-headed and responsible? Great, give them more than you initially thought wise, and tell them why you have done so. But what if you have doubts? Most of the time, I predict that your doubts will be unfounded and you'll be pleasantly surprised at how employees respond. A CIPD report published in October 2018 reveals that 37 per cent of employees felt they could cope with more demanding duties (based on a YouGov survey of a representative 3,700 employees, and CIPD's own focus groups). Give your people more trust than you may initially believe is justifiable. After all, most of your staff will have private lives that they manage well, why would they not manage your business well? And showing trust can boost job satisfaction and engagement levels. So not only will decisions be taken at lower levels, but those taking them will feel better. If you are unfortunate to have untrustworthy people, they will show themselves very quickly within the new culture, and then appropriate action can be taken.

4 *Cascade trust.* Having started at the top of the organization, trusted empowerment has to cascade through every layer of management. Push decision making about your targeted goals to lower levels. At every stage, the empowerment has to be defined and accepted by those being empowered. You may find that a small minority don't want to be empowered, and what will you do then? Think about your reaction before the start. And even when accepted, it may not mean that those empowered will act. What will you do then? Think about that issue as well before you begin.

5 *Big stuff as well.* You might want to start small, rolling out limited empowerment to test the reaction of those being empowered. Embed the adjustments if you receive a positive reaction, and then ask what additional responsibilities, authorities and powers would be acceptable to the community. Know that going further may meet more resistance, so pace the roll-out of more responsibilities to suit the audiences. Only accelerate the content when the employees have taken the whole initiative on-board mentally, and are asking for more.

6 *Training.* You cannot expect your people to embrace the concept without fully understanding the role that they have to play. They will need to be briefed about how the cascade system will work, the problems the people may confront, and the answers that may be needed. But the training is less about the theory and system, and far more about the mental and emotional adjustments the managers and staff are being asked to make. And you are always *asking* people for their cooperation. Telling people that they are empowered will have little effect. So invest in training workshops, role-play exercises simulating real-work situations before and after empowerment; and Q&A sessions with managers who need to ask, 'What do you think will be the problems when this thing goes live?' 'Please can you help to propose solutions to these problems?'

And don't be surprised if new tools are required as well; software modifications; new hardware; and don't forget that lack of relevant data may scupper the initiative on day one.

You can't ask people to make decisions without being able to access the knowledge upon which their decisions will be based.

7 *Pilot test.* Identify a few teams that you believe will be the first to 'give-it-a-go' with the new way of working and set up a pilot test to identify the problems that will constrain a more complete roll-out. Provide those teams with a communications feedback loop, or a notice board (virtual as well as actual), so that the staff can record problems as they happen. Escalations to higher authority levels will still be required on occasions, but too many, too frequently, will invalidate the whole exercise. Work through the reasons for escalations and modify the empowerment criteria if necessary to limit their occurrence.

8 *Limits and checks.* Re-define, and move out the 'points' and 'marks' beyond which employees may not step. Then you need to set up a system whereby individuals are assessed on their actions and decisions. Who is working to a new, higher limitation; who is carrying on as before; and who is exceeding their boundaries?

Nick Leeson brought down Barings Bank in 1995 because checks and balances were not in place. Contrast that with *Jidoka*, a Japanese term employed in Toyota's production system. According to the principles of the concept, a production line operator is empowered to take control and stop the production line if he or she determines that something is wrong or about to go wrong. It could be a health and safety issue or an equipment problem. Checks are established at every workstation and required of every employee. It goes without saying that regular checks must be made to ensure that employees are not doing anything wrong, but it is arguably more important to confirm that in the new empowered culture, people are exercising their newly granted powers.

9 *Budget.* In each management layer from the chief executive to the shop-floor supervisor, every manager will be both a winner and a loser. For example, a mid-level manager may be awarded additional powers, previously held by their immediate boss, but lose some powers that they had previously exercised, to their individual staff members. The cascading of power must be an uninterrupted flow through the organization's hierarchy. This will be a huge challenge to enterprises with a large workforce, both in terms of time and effort, but also money. The project team will need budget to define the changes and re-train everyone affected.

10 *Support.* An ongoing support structure may be needed because the managers of those that are suddenly empowered may feel disenfranchised and find it difficult to let go of their previous authority. Will they really hold back from doing what they previously did? Who will support them during the process? Some may feel that the whole reason for their value-add is being questioned; their jobs becoming insecure; and a structure to their working life removed. So the managers must be re-trained as well as their staff. What may prove uplifting and satisfying for the staff members may prove to be the opposite for their managers.

Earlier I referred to helicopter parents and to snowflakes. At work, the helicopter parent is re-named the micro-manager. Micro-managers hover and fuss over the progress of the employees' work, monitoring their every move, swooping in with instructions and telling stories of their previous successes whenever they think something may not be quite right. The manager's obsessive desire to know even the smallest detail of the work of their staff betrays their lack of self-confidence and concern about their own value to those above. These managers need a higher level of focus during the culture change as they will find it more difficult to abandon the equivalent of searching the travel bag for the toothbrush, or checking the oven temperature.

11 *Rewards.* Identify where the culture change of empowerment will be first noticeable. Is it in customer satisfaction; supplier attitudes and response times; or enterprise reputation? Ensure your survey data of the quality (key performance indicator) you are targeting is up to date and set a higher target but without a definite timeline. Setting a deadline can prove self-defeating and demoralizing if missed, and culture changes take more time than you initially plan. Extrinsic rewards should not be required as they should be trumped by the intrinsic.

A concluding story

Hamdi Ulukaya arrived in the United States over 20 years ago with less than $3,000 to his name. He was an immigrant from Turkey hoping to learn English and start a new life. Today he is a billionaire, owner of Chobani, a Greek yoghurt company that commands half of the yoghurt market in the US. After starting a small business buying and selling feta cheese, Mr Ulukaya bought an abandoned Kraft yoghurt factory in upstate New York. From the autumn of 2007 to 2012 he went from a handful of employees to thousands, and from zero to $1 billion in sales within those five years.

And what does Mr Ulukaya credit for his success? His people, whom he empowers in a variety of ways. In a 2018 *New York Times* article he was quoted as saying the following:

> Look, my background is a working-class background. And in the early days, I was a factory worker. One of my first dreams was to make this company a certain place where everybody's a partner, and they deserved a portion of what they have helped build. So I made a calculation. If you make $7 or $8 . . . an hour, you can't have a house. You can't have good food for your kids. Forget going on vacation. The math just doesn't make sense. And I look at it from the bigger perspective. Especially for rural communities, I don't see any other way of finding a long-term solution than businesses stepping up, for their own employees and especially for their own communities. We have to start worrying about our own employees, their families and their children's well-being, and the school, and the firehouse, and the baseball field.[6]

This is a lesson for all of us, whether in the boardroom or the bedroom, we can always do more by empowering those around us and leading every day of our lives by maintaining our distance and intervening only when required.

Question. Decide upon areas where you could exercise more power, then ask for it. Then decide which of your own powers could be delegated to someone else.

I want more power in these areas	I could delegate these powers to others

The Everyday Leader delegates real power to those closest, recognizing that they will make mistakes and that the leader will have to pick up the pieces.
The Everyday Leader demonstrates that empowerment starts at the top and sets a good example.
The Everyday Leader advances an empowerment agenda with support and training where needed.

13

Leading whistleblowing

Everyday leaders fall into one or more classifications when dealing with whistleblowing: They could be the ones blowing the whistle; they could be helping and advising a colleague or friend to report perceived wrongdoings; or they could be designing or administering a whistleblowing policy or procedure. I'll examine all three and try to offer some advice. First, let us define what whistleblowing actually means.

What is (and isn't) whistleblowing?

What is whistleblowing and who qualifies as a whistleblower? The UK government defines a whistleblower as someone working inside an organization, who reports certain types of wrongdoing. This will usually be something they've seen at work, although it could be outside of the workplace, providing that what is reported is in the public interest, e.g. a criminal offence that could adversely affect others. Whistleblowers are theoretically protected by law if i) there is a danger to health and safety; ii) a risk or actual damage to the environment; iii) someone is covering up for serious mistakes or wrongdoing; or iv) if an organization is breaking the law. And there is no express time limit for reporting something that happened in the past. Even agency workers and workers on temporary contracts are protected.

Personal grievances such as alleged discrimination, bullying, harassment do not normally count as whistleblowing under UK law unless the complaint is part of a systematic practice and in the public interest to investigate. Otherwise, these types of complaints should be raised in accordance with the organization's own policies and procedures or with statutory employment laws.

Clearly risk to life and limb is in the public interest, so problems with hospitals, doctors, nurses, pilots etc. come top of the list. Let's have a look at a few examples and as you read, imagine the stress with which these everyday leaders have had to cope with knowledge that was not privy to the general public. And ask yourself whether you too have the nerve (I wanted to use another word starting with 'b' but my publisher vetoed it) to be a whistleblower?

Some notable examples of whistleblowing

Right from the start of her campaign in 2008, Julie Bailey was getting anonymous hate mail. Why? She was the person who blew the whistle on Mid-Staffordshire Hospital in central England, for what she saw as gross negligence and cruelty in the treatment of her mum, Bella, who was 86 at the time. You would have thought that the local population would have been supportive of her efforts to improve the way patients were treated at the hospital. But no. Her exposure of the hospital's culture of neglect and harm was profoundly unpopular in some quarters. After the emergency department was closed at night pending review, she says, the abuse got worse: 'I was getting cards saying, "I hope you die in an ambulance on the way to hospital now you have closed this one." I had my car tyres slashed, "Bitch" written on my windows, and "Shut your f . . . ing mouth"'.

A public inquiry led by Robert Francis QC published in 2013 damned the absence of 'care, compassion, humanity and leadership' at 'all levels' of the NHS trust. Almost every sentence of its judgment was a vindication of Bailey's outrage. Julie is a strong and determined character, but she paid a high price for her campaign, ostracized by some and virtually driven out of town for her decision to 'blow the whistle' on the local hospital where many of her (former) friends and neighbours were employed. Those who have interests in maintaining the status quo can prove powerful opponents to those interested in advancing the public good. But what intrigues me is how the staff at the hospital, the doctors, nurses, administration professionals and even patients kept quiet. For years. Who knows how many people died as a result?[1]

British Airways pilot, Julian Monaghan, 49, was jailed for eight months in 2018, for being almost six times over the limit for alcohol as he prepared to take off for Mauritius with 300 passengers on board. The whistleblower was a flight technician who smelt alcohol on the pilot's breath as he entered the cockpit. Well done to the flight technician for demonstrating and illustrating everyday leadership even though she was below the administrative rank of the pilot. But there were signs that other pilots saw evidence of heavy drinking and did not report it for investigation. It was also reported that a cleaner working in the pilots' shared accommodation became concerned after frequently clearing up empty vodka bottles, but was dissuaded from reporting her observations by her colleagues. Lots of people had serious suspicions. But there was no everyday leadership until that one person – the flight technician – stepped up to the plate and made a difference. If you were one of the other pilots that had been made aware of the cleaner's concerns, what would have been your response? Would you:

1. Do nothing, say nothing.
2. Mention your concerns to other captains and rely on their judgements
3. Raise your concerns directly with Julian Monaghan, starting with, 'I feel that there is a potential problem . . .' Expect the brush-off and persevere with your interaction. 'If there is a problem, know that you can get help.' Tell Julian of the company's procedures and sources of external help. Tell him not to threaten his career when help is available etc.
4. Report your suspicions directly to officials of British Airways.

Pilots carry huge responsibilities every time they fly. Passengers expect them to be at the top of their game. Covering up potentially dangerous behaviour from them seems difficult to explain. Understandable yes, because it would seem to others that someone is betraying a colleague. But Julian needed help and didn't get it. Now he is in jail. If only someone had emerged as a whistleblower earlier, Julian may have been spared such an awful fate.

Russian whistleblower Yuliya Stepanova is still in hiding after helping to expose Russian state-sponsored doping at the Olympic games. Russia was suspended by the International Association of Athletics Federations (IAAF) in November 2015 after an independent World Anti-Doping Agency (WADA) report depicted a culture of widespread doping.

Yuliya and her husband Vitaly, a former Russian anti-doping official, had to move to a secret location following her evidence to WADA's report into Russian doping. 'In our current location we do feel safe, but unfortunately the reaction to our actions in our home country is not positive, a lot of people in general, and athletes as well, hate us for what we did and we would not go back to Russia right now. There we would feel unsafe.'

There are many countries where whistleblowers face punishment, even death. Everyday leaders in dangerous situations should be ultra-careful before putting the whistle to their mouths. If their situation warrants, they should have an escape plan; secret hide-outs booked and money deposited where it can be easily accessed. But most importantly they shouldn't go it alone; involve many other people who can be trusted absolutely.

Journalist Daphne Caruana Galizia, 53, was murdered in an apparently targeted bomb attack on her car in 2017. She lived on the beautiful island of Malta and had posted previous entries on her blog which highlighted cases of alleged high-level corruption in her country. Politicians of all persuasions were particular targets of her writing and Daphne was relentless. Her killing sparked furious protests on the island, with thousands marching against what some called the 'mafia state'. Her family let it be known that they did not want the country's Prime Minister or President to attend her funeral. Both had been Daphne's targets.

From Malta to the UK, and to the mistrusted finance sector. Barclays Bank boss, Jes Staley has had to pay over £1.1 million in fines as punishment for his attempts to unmask an internal bank whistleblower who sent letters to the bank raising concerns about the appointment of a senior executive. Staley admitted that he made a mistake and kept his job. For a very rich person, Jes can afford the fine, but does the punishment set a poor example for other potential whistleblower trackers? This was more than a throw-away remark such as, 'find out who did this'. Investigation by the authorities found that Barclays' security people pressurised the US Postal Service to look at CCTV to try to identify the person posting the letters.

Staley said: 'I have consistently acknowledged that my personal involvement in this matter was inappropriate and I have apologised for mistakes which I made.' At the following annual general meeting, one investor said this to the Chairman: 'The chief executive is irrevocably tarnished. I suggest you consider his continuation.' However, the MP Nicky Morgan, chair of the House of Commons Treasury committee, said she planned to question the Financial Conduct Authority (FCA) about the fine: 'As the FCA's decision notice states, a [CEO] should set an example to the firm's employees.' Clearly, Mr Staley has failed in this regard. Reputation stained. Permanently.

This was yet another case of 'doing the not-so-right-thing, hope there isn't too much fall-out, and we might get away with it' philosophy, which is extremely risky. This gamble could have cost Jes Stanley his job and employability in the finance sector. And there are several commentators who still think it should have done.

Options for the everyday whistleblower

The examples above showcase that the world of whistleblowing can be rather dangerous. Speak up and bad things could happen. Keep quiet and bad things could happen. It's the proverbial Catch-22 or Gordian knot – any way you pull, you might be tightening the noose.

What to do?

Let's take a look at the data produced by a UK whistleblowing charity called 'Protect', previously called 'Public Concern at Work' (PCAW). They released a five-year review, 'Whistleblowing: Time for Change' in 2016, an update on their 2011 report. 'Protect' operate a free and confidential advice line to workers unsure of whether, or how, to raise a concern. They receive 2000–2500 calls per year. Here are their headline findings:

- 25 per cent increase in the number of calls received since 2011;
- 68 per cent of callers start by raising their concerns openly;
- 9 per cent raised a matter confidentially;
- 2 per cent remained anonymous;
- 69 per cent had tried to raise a concern but were ignored by those higher-up before they contacted 'Protect';
- four out of five whistleblowers reported a negative outcome, such as:
    - 29 per cent of whistleblowers were themselves victimized
    - 28 per cent were dismissed
    - 24 per cent resigned
    - 2 per cent were bullied.

The top three types of concerns over the five years were:

- financial malpractice;
- ethical decision-making; and
- patient/customer safety.

Knowing these figures, it is perhaps no surprise so few of us actually are the ones to bring to light a possible transgression. If you spot something wrong, an internal battle starts between two competing voices within you, the one telling you to forget it and move on and the one saying if not you, then who? Which voice will you act upon? Report or not report?

Before you answer, think about this advice from 'Protect':

- Is there a colleague, supervisor or senior manager you trust that can approach with your concerns?
- Can you find a solution within the broader community or team?
- Are there others who are willing to speak up with you?
- Does your organization have a whistleblowing policy?
- Have you sought advice from any other source? (a union, an advisory body or solicitor)

Practical tips for the everyday whistleblower

Here are some practical tips for raising a whistleblowing concern:

- *Let the facts speak for themselves.* Concentrate on the facts of a situation and focus on what you know for sure. Relying on hearsay and rumour may upset or anger your colleagues and/or employer and may damage personal reputations and work relationships. Remember there may be an innocent or good explanation for what has occurred.
- *Separate out personal grievances.* A public concern and a personal grievance are not the same thing. If you are aggrieved about your personal position, you should use your employer's internal grievance procedure to make this known. If you are unsure which category your concern falls into, seek advice.
- *Be a witness not a complainant.* Communicate the concern in a professional, calm and factual manner. If you know how to resolve the problem, suggest a solution. As a witness you do not have to prove your concern and it is important you do not delay raising the concern by acting as a private detective.

'Protect' has published a number of true-life case studies. Here is one example: 'M' was an experienced secondary school teacher who was approached by staff members who were concerned that exam results were being falsified. After seeing some of the evidence, M raised the concern with the head teacher. As a result, M was subjected to a campaign of victimization from top management. M contacted 'Protect' (then PCAW) for advice and support and given the strength of this claim and the seriousness of the concerns, PCAW managed to secure pro bono legal support for him. M subsequently settled his claim. These were M's thoughts on the experience when PCAW spoke to him a few months after his claim had settled:

> I don't know what motivates most people to speak up. I hope it's a sense that something is wrong. Any other reason would give whistleblowers a bad name. Certainly in my case it was an incredible sense of injustice, an intense feeling of wrongness, that I had to tell someone about it. If I am really honest, I would have to question whether I would advise myself to do it again bearing in mind the consequences that have flowed from my decision to blow the whistle. I would like to think I would but I cannot guarantee it. What I wish I had done differently is to put everything in writing right from the word go. I also wish I had familiarized myself with the policies and procedures at work.

Setting up proper whistleblowing policies

This last sentence in M's reflections, speaks to the importance of those in leadership positions anticipating that sometimes people make poor choices and bad decisions and outcomes follow. So you need policies in place to protect those who become aware of these transgressions. If you are or will be involved in the design or administration of a whistleblowing policy or procedure then 'Protect' offers advice around three core elements:

- *Governance*: Accountability, written policy and procedures, review and reporting.
- *Engagement*: Communications and training.
- *Operations:* Support and protection, recording and investigations, resolution and feedback.

And within each core element there are a series of best practice standards to aim for.

Encouraging others to come forward with whistleblowing information

Your customers

Customers can be whistleblowers too, but this needs to be separated from 'customer feedback'. I have known many companies who profess to take customer satisfaction seriously, and become focused on the 'minutiae' of customer complaints. Is it just me, or we being asked to complete a satisfaction survey with almost every purchase that we make these days? Television adverts proudly claim to be five-star rated and websites feature reviews from the satisfied and disaffected. I, and I suspect like you, don't believe or trust in most of them, and I don't waste my time doing surveys. Everyday leaders have to spend their time more profitably.

But for a moment, let's assume that you truly become concerned about whistleblowing customers, community colleagues or family members. What should you do?

In terms of customers, you may be tempted to order the following directive: 'In order to get the number of complaints down, let's target managers with an objective.' Superficially, that sounds like a reasonable thing to do, but it's wrong. Managers and operators know how to hit targets and deliver the requested performance outcomes to their bosses. I can hear clever managers asking, 'What is a complaint exactly?' Is there a specific definition or do individuals decide for themselves? Is this a complaint: 'The product works well but it was late arriving'? 'No, I didn't think so, either. OK team, let's stop counting late arrivals as a complaint and instead only track the complaints with the product itself.' Not the outcome you anticipated as a leader.

The reason is that by setting a goal that asks for a reduction in complaints, you will get the answer you wanted, but unfortunately, you, the everyday leader will be no wiser as to the root causes of dissatisfaction. This is an example of the well-known, and all too often observed scenario explained by Professor Steven Kerr in his famous article entitled, 'On the folly of rewarding A, while hoping for B.'[2]

So, if you find yourself in these circumstances, and want to truly improve underlying customer loyalty and well-being, then you should consider targeting *an increase* in customer complaints. This may appear to be counter-intuitive, but you can see why, can't you? You want to encourage your workers to dig deep and not cover up problems. As a leader you may start to discover the underlying reality of how the organization actually performs or doesn't perform on the ground (i.e., do we have a good product, but delivery needs attention?). Better still for managers to hear directly and honestly from customers, to get out and meet customers personally, even if it means having to travel far and wide to do so.

I know that one very large company, a household name in the UK, insists that an executive director dons the headset and answers incoming customer complaint calls every Friday. The duty rotates between a small group of directors, who benefit from gaining first-hand knowledge of customer perceptions and insights. This is corporate gold dust that is normally swept under the rug by lower-level employees fearing repercussions from top management. By encouraging senior executives to listen to customers, this is a signal to frontline employees that their concerns and those of the customers they hear from matter to the firm. Moreover, by being close to the action, management can do something about the issue immediately.

Normally I don't complain, but last May I did so personally to Bill Marriott, head of the Mariott chain of hotels, after extremely disappointing visits to two of his hotels. A swift and welcome response from his office was followed up by a personal contact with the managers of the two hotels concerned. They apologized and both invited my wife and I back for a complimentary night in an attempt to put things right. But they did more. They explained fully why we did not get the service we had expected and the corrective actions they had taken.

Personal connection, apology and recompense. Good job. But supposing my wife didn't complain, simply decided never to visit a Marriott again. The most worrying trend for all organizations are the large number of customers who leave, who defect without complaining, or in the words of the late Albert O. Hirschman, choose 'exit over voice'.[3] Hirschman shows quite persuasively in his 1972 book – still relevant today – *Exit, Voice, and Loyalty: Responses to Decline in Firms, Organizations, and States*, that you block voice at your peril.

You may profit and, literally, save your company from certain death by trying to follow-up the non-returning customers, the ones who may have blown the whistle silently, and not placed an order with you ever again.

Your neighbours and community

Next let's examine how you interact with your neighbours and community colleagues.

- Situation 1: Your neighbour, George, tells you that he's noticed a lot of different people (all men) visiting a house just a few doors down from yours during the daytime that is occupied by a single mum.
- Situation 2: Your neighbour, Priti, is collecting evidence of who may be involved locally in drug dealing and asks for your support.
- Situation 3: You have been told by your neighbour Kuldip that a local religious leader seems to be attempting to brainwash some young people.

All three are blowing the whistle, and they are coming to you, a single parent with a job and two kids to raise on your own, to join them in doing something.

Your options in the first situation are:

1 Do nothing. Live and let live.

2 Visit during the day and share with your neighbour a few doors down, the information you received. 'Just thought I'd let you know that tongues are wagging and people are making the most negative judgements about you and the number of men calling on you. I hope everything is OK?'

3 Listen, observe and collect your own sample data before deciding how to proceed. The single mum may be being

exploited by others and needs help from the authorities; or she may be dealing drugs and the police need to be notified. Or, totally innocent, she is a counsellor working from a home office, helping alcoholics (mostly men) kick the habit.

4 Add your own option here: ....

What would you as the everyday leader do?

Now what about the response to Priti regarding her concerns about drug-dealing in the neighbourhood:

1 Do nothing. Live and let live.

2 Agree that you will monitor the neighbourhood activities more closely and report your observations to her.

3 Join with Priti in her efforts and help to lead the response.

4 Add your own option here: ....

What would you as the everyday leader do?

Now finally, dealing with the reports of attempted brainwashing:

1 Do nothing. You don't want to get involved.

2 Share your information with others on social media asking for any additional observations and reported meetings.

3 Report the information you have received to the police and local schools.

4 Add your own option here: ....

What would you the everyday leader do?

Your own household

Finally, let us bring this whole whistleblowing thing back home. What about family members who come to you with areas of concern? Specifically, concerns about things occurring in your home. How would you react and respond as the person to whom these whistleblowing concerns were raised?

1. Situation 1: Your daughter tells you that your partner has been drinking and smells of booze when you are not around.
2. Situation 2: Your partner tells you that one of your children is becoming more withdrawn and monosyllabic in response to questions and fears a mental health challenge is emerging.
3. Situation 3: Your daughter tells you that she thinks her best friend's father is becoming violent at home.

Although not everyday challenges, I ask you to think about how you would respond to the first situation. You could say:

- 'Don't worry sweetheart, all of us have a stressful time now and then and we're allowed to enjoy a glass or two to unwind.'

  Or

- 'Thank you for bringing that to my attention sweetheart. Don't worry. I'll have a word and find out what's going on.'

  Or

- Confronting your partner, 'Mikey says that you smell of booze. What's going on?'

Or

- Add your own option here: ....

The second challenge could be handled by saying:

- 'Don't worry sweetheart, she's at a difficult age and everyone gets a bit down now and again.'

  Or

- 'We have to find out if there is anything that's worrying her. How do you think we should proceed?'

  Or

- Talking to your daughter directly by saying: 'Gemma, Dad says that you have become withdrawn and look unhappy these days. What's wrong, angel?'

  Or

- Add your own option here: ....

Finally, in response to the third situation you could say:

- 'Oh no, I hope not, darling. Why do you think that? What signs have you noticed?'

  Or

- 'I'd better talk to her mother when we next meet.'

  Or

- 'Let me know when she next visits, and I'll have a word with her myself.'

Or

- Add your own option here: ....

What would the everyday leader do?

A whistleblowing policy for your family?

Before we end, have you talked about whistleblowing in general terms to all of your family members? Have you given them some guidance? I do not want to worry you unnecessarily if you are a parent of teenagers, but at the end of 2014, a shocking statistic appeared deep in the pages of a World Health Organization (WHO) report. It was this: suicide has become the leading killer of teenage girls, worldwide. It is also a leading cause of death in young men.

How would you lead a family discussion about this very sensitive subject? Maybe borrowing some techniques from the whistleblowing literature, you can begin opening up or reinforcing channels of communication. Once established, you can refer to a local or national suicide and enquire of your child or children if the subject is discussed at their school. Then you can lead the conversation nearer to home. Good luck.

Question. List as many 'signs' of potential wrong doing by an individual, and by an organization that you may be aware of. Look to see if they rise above a personal grievance to the potential whistleblowing threshold of harming others and/or society-at-large. If so, it may be time for you to consider your options.

By an individual	By a team or organization

The Everyday Leader thanks those who bring a potential wrong-doing to their notice and initiates an investigation, however informal or however uncomfortable to those implicated and/or affected.
The Everyday Leader doesn't trivialize or make an excuse when potential wrong-doing is brought to their attention.

14

Leading change

Does this book really need a separate chapter on leading change as all of the previous chapters were, in one sense or another, all about change? I believe it does so that I can highlight the common threats and difficulties that need to be addressed when initiating change within a family environment or a large organization, and to offer some recommendations for your consideration.

Things that are common to all change initiatives

People do not like to change, and as a corollary neither do organizations. There are always exceptions, but if you, as the everyday leader want to introduce change, then be aware that the majority of people have an emotional attachment to the status quo, however harmful that may be to them.

Many readers may not have been born when Coca Cola changed the formula (and look) of its famous soda back in 1985. All hell broke loose amongst the supporters of the original formula. Fans complained to the media, petitions were started, and national campaigns organized to save 'old' Coke. After 77 days of world-wide protests the consumers won. The Company gave in and reverted to the original formula. The Company said later that it had learned a powerful lesson: It was the consumers that 'owned the brand' and not the Company that made it.

Emotional attachment is a powerful force, and often it can be harnessed to the detriment of those wanting to change the status quo.

Organizations are social enterprises, and hence like the individual stakeholders that constitute them, they are difficult to change. In the 1970s Marks and Spencer ruled the retail high street in the UK, with a slogan of 'quality, value, choice'. It made over £1 billion profit well into the 1990s, but it didn't react fast enough to the threats from competitors and the emerging internet and online shopping phenomenon. Today, its clothing business is a fraction of what it used to be, and only in 2020, will its customers enjoy the opportunity to do a food shop online, a full 24 years after Tesco introduced the concept.

So change too fast without notice – like Coca Cola did in 1985 – and you're sunk, or don't change fast enough – like Marks and Spencer on the cusp of the new millennium – and you're sunk. It seems like a proverbial Catch-22 all over again. Well actually, it's not that simple. Let's walk through some of the constants involved in change (contradictory pun intended)!

Anchoring effects

If you play the national or state lottery, you probably use the same numbers week after week, year after year, don't you? And most likely you meet with no success, but do you change the numbers? Probably not, because you say to yourself, 'Supposing I change the numbers and then they come up?'

Alone on a train, you go to the lavatory and when you return, someone has taken 'your' seat. 'Excuse me, that's my seat,' you might be tempted to say. Even though there may be plenty of other seats available, you want 'your' seat back. You don't want to change and you are not alone.

The late Amos Tversky and Nobel Prize Laureate Daniel Khaneman hit upon the idea that when people are reacting to changes or trying to make a decision, they often use an anchor or focal point as a reference or starting point.[1] Psychologists have found that people have a tendency to rely (often too much so) on the very first piece of information they encounter or the very first experience they engage in, which can have a noticeable effect on the ultimate decisions they end up making. In psychology, this type of cognitive bias is known as 'anchoring'.

The 'anchoring effect' or 'incumbency bias' was at work in all the situations cited above, and it works in many situations. If a store places a large price on an item, and then underneath shows by how much it is 'slashing the price', this can compel someone to buy the item even if they had not intended to buy it at that time, since customers tend to decide on amounts skewed towards the anchor value, in this case the original price. Anchoring can also affect wage negotiations and bargaining between parties. Setting a wage offer that is known to be 'too low' might normally deter a union from agreeing to a contract. However, when the employer then agrees to a higher wage after a period of 'back-and-forth bargaining' (which may be the wage they had actually intended to pay the workers all along), the original lower wage offer serves as an anchor, making the new wage seem like a much better deal.

A well-known example of the power of anchoring is an advertisement, cited in a number of business marketing textbooks, run by the magazine *The Economist*, which offered three subscription options: a web-only subscription, which cost $59; a print-only subscription, which cost $125; or both web and print, which also cost $125. Given these options, no subjects chose the print-only subscription, which was the clearly inferior option, and a majority chose the dual print and web subscription for $125. That seems perfectly logical. However, when they removed the print-only option for $125, the majority of people chose the web-only subscription for $59. Even though nobody was interested in the print-only option, having it listed as an 'option' served as an anchor to make the more expensive, dual subscription seem like a much better deal.

Overcoming anchors and gaining acceptance for change

Whilst there is often resistance to change in many circumstances, in other situations large communities demand it. Tony Blair secured his first victory in 1997 against John Major, ushering in the first Labour government in Britain in more than two decades. Obama's campaign used the slogan 'Change we can believe in' and the chant 'Yes We Can'. Out with the old, in with the new. Americans and Brits wanted a change and got it, so things can and do eventually change.

For you, the everyday leader, making changes and initiating them with those around you (your colleagues, family and friends) is a big challenge. At home, only an effective parent can lead their children away from drugs or gangs or towards a healthier lifestyle and get them to accept the 'rightness' of the proposed action. Only an effective boss at work can swing an organization away from its focus on procedures, process and technology and towards an acceptance of the customer as the driving force of major decision making. And only an effective religious head can ask communities to reject bigotry and accept an understanding of opposing ideas and ideologies.

The important word here is 'accept'. Ineffective leaders often make changes, which are not accepted, making changes by diktat that never truly materialize. That can create more problems than the change was endeavouring to solve. So the next time you, as the everyday leader, are trying to rally people around a decision, or reacting negatively to a perceived change in the status quo, give a little thought to the possible impact of the anchoring bias on peoples choices and feelings about the change in question. Are you giving enough consideration to all of the available information and all of the possible options, or are you focusing too heavily on an existing anchor point?

Elements of a successful change process

There are plenty of books available on change processes, but in my experience, the following elements are critical when attempting change:

- establish credibility;
- confront the brutal truth;

- justify the change to the whole community, family or work colleagues;
- name a project manager and their contact details;
- communicate the change process, stage 1, stage 2 etc.;
- set the example yourself, by making obvious and well-publicized adjustments;
- correct wrong behaviours consistently and even-handedly;
- publically acknowledge and celebrate adherence/compliance to the new way;
- resource generously with people and money. It will cost a lot more than you think;
- publicize your change programme widely; and finally
- include a helpline contact/number, or in the case of family, take regular time-outs with your children.

Let's walk through each of the elements above, with examples and explanations.

Establish credibility

Establishing credibility and expertise is crucial in all situations. At home, you say to your kids, 'Stop swearing' to which they may reply, 'But you swear.' Or you may tell your partner, who is in a very stressful job, to stop smoking, while you, semi-retired, continue to smoke in social situations.

If you have given up swearing and smoking and your kids or your partner needs advice, you have earned credibility by your previous efforts. You can be an everyday leader.

But you can't be an everyday leader inspiring change if, like Scarlett Moffat a reality-show minor celebrity, you lose a lot of weight by jetting off to Switzerland for a rapid weight-loss boot camp of exercise and low calorie intake, and then claim, in your newly released fitness video, that the weight loss was caused by following the DVD routine you are hawking.

By contrast though, the parable of a famous leader, often cited as Nasrudin (from the thirteenth century) or Mahatma Gandhi, and sugar, sets a terrific example. I have heard this story many times, in different versions attributed to different people, but the basics are the same. For the purposes of retelling the story I will use Gandhi. A woman was worried about the excessive amounts of sugar her son was consuming and the damaging effect this was having on his teeth. No amount of lecturing or hectoring had any effect, so in desperation she took her son to see Gandhi, and asked him to tell the child to stop eating sugar. He told them to come back in two weeks and so, frustrated, she returned home. A fortnight later, the mother and son revisited Gandhi who told the boy to stop eating sugar. The boy, recognizing the importance of Ghandi's words, promised that he would.

But before turning away, the woman asked why Gandhi did not tell her son to stop eating sugar two weeks ago. Ghandi's reply was: 'Because two weeks ago I was still eating sugar myself, and I needed time to stop before speaking to your child.'

Much like the story of Geoff Whitington and his two sons in Chapter 3, you can't ask someone to stop doing something that you yourself are still doing. Neither can you ask someone to start doing something that you haven't started to do. Otherwise you're not credible.

Some organizations make huge mistakes with change and damage their credibility. Daimler bought Chrysler in the early 2000s and then offloaded it to Fiat. HP bought Autonomy and very soon after, started legal proceedings against the previous CEO and CFO. Homebase, once part of the Argos empire, was sold to Wesfarmers, an Australian company in 2016 for a reported £340 million. Immediately, they replaced the senior and middle managers with their own staff, and started to re-badge Homebase with their own 'Bunnings' brand. Disaster followed disaster – for example, barbecues arrived at the start of winter – and losses mounted; two years later, the company was sold for £1. Wesfarmers made an estimated A$1 billion loss on the whole enterprise.

Confront the brutal truth

'We're standing on a burning platform,' said Stephen Elop in Chapter 9; in effect saying that the basis for their business has been severely eroded and they have to change in order to have a future. The full wording of the memo was very direct. He asked his employees to imagine that a man was working on an oil rig in the North Sea when he was awoken by a loud explosion which set the whole platform on fire. He stated that the man managed to scramble to the edge of the rig and looked down at the icy waters 30m below. The choices are stark. Stay on the platform and be consumed by fire or jump and risk death by drowning or hypothermia? Whatever your deep-seated concerns are, at some point you have to confront the brutal truth, however difficult that may be, and especially so with loved ones.

Anthony and Ian Whitington confronted the reality of their situation with their dad. But what if one of your children is being bullied at school or on social media and is hesitant or afraid to confront it? Supposing your child is questioning their sexuality as a teenager?

For them, starting a serious conversation with you is always difficult when conversations at home are usually about trivia and minor logistics. Imagine how difficult it will be for them to raise a worrying issue when the family is discussing what to eat for dinner? So how about agreeing on a signal with your child when he or she wants to talk seriously about something that is troubling him/her? Can he or she put something obvious on their bedroom door? Or offer you a pre-agreed object or book as a sign? For them, signals will be a lot easier than words. The everyday leader has to make the start of the conversation easy.

Justify the change to the whole community, family or work colleagues

Elucidate the problem before promoting the solution. Be open with data and with feelings. Imagine that you have been offered another job, which means either a long commute or a house move that will affect the whole family and close relatives. Make everyone aware of the situation in as many different ways as you can. Get them involved by asking for their ideas and suggestions before making a decision. If you decide to move home, then be open about the feelings of loss and the subsequent compensatory factors. Some will embrace change quickly, others resist strongly. In your mind, list them in order, with the most resistant last. Why? Because I recommend that you work on them individually, starting with the most amenable to change. Once those are convinced, they will act as your surrogate, your deputy – selling the new ways to other family members in your absence.

Name a project manager and their contact details

In May 2018 a new timetable was introduced for large parts of Britain's railway network, which caused major disruption to train services; frequent cancellations; customer fury; and eventually a government public enquiry into the chaos. The investigation found that 'nobody was in charge'. The new timetable was proposed and prepared in 2017, and designed to take advantage of improvements to the rail network infrastructure, but the inquiry found that there was and is 'an apparent gap in industry responsibility and accountability for managing systemic risks'.[2] Even in September 2018, customers were still suffering an unreliable and expensive service, and overcrowded trains. Many commuters have since taken to the roads instead, causing yet more congestion, frustration and anger. No one came forward and said, 'It's all my fault.' The project lacked a competent, powerful and authoritative leader who commanded the respect of all concerned.

The lesson here is simple: make sure your changes have a highly visible lead figure, someone who has the authority to order any unforeseen, but necessary, modifications to the change programme.

Communicate the change process, stage 1, stage 2, etc.

You will need time before the change is introduced. Time to prepare the ground for success. But unfortunately many changes are mandated from on high with very little time between the announcement and the actual change. 'Well let's just get it done!' is heard more often than not. Unless urgency is needed for safety issues, taking time to communicate and brief those affected will encourage their participation. Those higher in the organization may be unaware of the small details known only to those lower down, and which may have an unforeseen negative impact on the roll-out. I would be surprised if their input didn't improve the plan in some way.

A catastrophic failure of a computer system in May 2018 deprived nearly 2 million customers of TSB bank of their online financial services, and opened them up to identity theft. The UK retail bank had tried to transfer its customers onto a new platform without rigorous pre-testing and a pilot trial. Over 12,000 customers closed their accounts; it cost the chief executive his job and the company over £100 million in damages.[3]

Let as many people as feasibly possible get involved in the details of a change initiative so that they can spot the weaknesses before they become serious pitfalls. Open the communication channels.

Set the example yourself, by making obvious and well-publicized adjustments

If you ask your child or children to reduce the time they spend on their mobile phones or laptops, then you have to lead the way and stop using yours. Seems obvious, but examples of hypocrisy are not just amusing but prolific. For example, when doctors offer their advice on quitting smoking cigarettes, and then nip around the back of the building to have a quick drag.

In Chapter 4, I described how Mike Coupe, the boss of the Sainsbury's supermarket group, was to receive a proposed 42 per cent pay rise whilst asking his lower level staff to forgo long-held benefits. The everyday leader would cancel those same benefits for themselves and order the same reductions for the most senior directors.

At Addenbrooke's Hospital, car parking for staff has become a big issue, as some staff are going to be denied the car space they have enjoyed previously, often for many years. I have seen the email sent out to staff and it doesn't mention the fact that the most senior medical and administrative managers have given up their own spaces. If they have, they should have mentioned it in the email, and if they haven't, they should do so and voluntarily offer their spaces to more junior colleagues. Set the example of the change you wish to lead.

When Sky News were looking for a new campaign for change to promote on their network in 2016, Helen-Ann Smith gave her boss four options: tackling pollution of the oceans by discarded plastic; organ transplant sign-up; more cyclists to wear helmets; and more beds in the NHS for teenagers needing urgent mental support. After more research and much discussion, 'Ocean Rescue'[4] was born in January 2017. Sky was attempting to do-good, but it needed to set the example if their campaign was to be taken seriously. When I met with John Ryley, the Head of Sky News at their HQ to learn more about their campaign, I drank water from a metal can as plastic cups had been banned; I used metal cutlery in their canteen; and food was served in non-plastic containers. Not only has Sky News set the example but they have asked all of their suppliers to be free of single-use plastic within two years. John told me that not only has their campaign attracted widespread support and been acknowledged as being worthwhile, but it has secured new connections and support from organizations that otherwise may have been more difficult for Sky to establish. Evidence that the vast majority of people want to do the right thing and respond positively to individuals and organizations who are willing to accept a small risk and take the lead.

Correct wrong behaviours consistently and even-handedly

Some people resist the change that they are being asked to make. And by that I mean, those individuals who have to stop doing stuff. It's likely that they will feel the loss emotionally, because whatever they did, they did with a sense of pride, and they thought it was important. They were proud of their work. And they will try to hang on to the intrinsic rewards they earned previously from it. The everyday leader acknowledges this, and helps individuals through their emotional journey, but always calls for corrections when individuals step away from the new method or system.

Managers are not exempt from hanging on to the past. I have often heard this from senior executives: 'We have to penetrate the (insert choice of permafrost, concrete, clay, or sponge layer) of middle management.' This means that whatever message is sent down to effect change gets blocked, either intentionally or unintentionally, by those tasked with making the change. Even US Presidents are not immune to the same resistance. Bill Clinton once said, 'Being president is like running a cemetery; you've got a lot of people under you and nobody's listening.'

But there may come a time, when, after more training, more support, and more encouragement that your patience begins to wear a little thin. Then you may need to ask the 'resisters', the 'non-listeners' if they want to be re-allocated to a different role. But do not waver from promoting the change as absolutely necessary, stating your full support for it.

Acknowledge and celebrate publicly, adherence and compliance to the new way

Search for early wins so that you can publicize the successes and praise the individuals who have accepted the changes you have instigated. The so-called 'early-adopters' are very important as they may act as your 'agents of change'. In your absence, their colleagues watch them and see for themselves that your changes are being actioned. If people need to be physically relocated then do it as soon as practicable. A new environment, especially if you are able to improve the surroundings (even if it is just a lick of paint) can accelerate the adoption of new procedures and practices.

If progress is much slower than you had anticipated, bring the team or teams together regularly and discuss their concerns openly. Staff are usually quick to spot flaws in the proposed solution: 'I tried to access the new data, but couldn't.' 'It took ages for x to happen, so I went back to our old way.' List their concerns and have a response ready for the next get-together. Much of thc talk will be about operational issues, but encourage them to talk about their feelings as well.

Resource generously with people and money

Everyone has experienced change, either in a family or at work as an operator or as a manager. And if your experience is anything like the norm, those changes will have taken longer and cost more than originally predicted. Change will cost a lot more than you think.

The UK television show, Grand Designs, has been running for about 20 years and in every episode, a husband and wife team embark upon a major renovation of an existing building or design their own house and commission its construction. The presenter of the show,

Kevin McCloud, always asks for the budget they have available and an estimate of the time they believe it will take. The actual final costs and timelines have been over-run in over 95 per cent of cases that I have watched, sometimes so disastrously that work either has to stop, or family loans or credit cards have to be used to complete the work.

These people were not naïve; they just could not have foreseen all of the unexpected groundwork discoveries or structural problems. Neither can you in your change programme, so make your calculations as carefully as you can and arrive at an exact figure, but always use a generous range for the outcome in all communications: 'I estimate the changes, including re-training to be in the range of £200–300k.'

Publicize your change programme widely and include a help-line number, or time-out with your children

One of my Grandsons has changed his afternoon schedule of work. Instead of finishing school, completing his homework and then going to the tennis courts, he finishes school, goes to the sports centre café to relax and unwind before he hits a few balls, and only then completes his homework. His mum and his tennis coach have had to adjust their diary commitments and time allocations for other things. I urged all three to record their feelings day-by-day after the change. Looking back through their logs all of them can see how they have individually come to accept that the changes were for the best. Only by logging daily times, weights, distances, etc. can athletes see their own progress. So it is with your change programme at work. Get the data out to everyone and chart progress.

I would urge you to avoid snappy new slogans unless the people affected have been directly involved in their design and development. A short slogan has a tendency to put people off and trivialise the issue. 'Who on earth thought of that one?' will be the response on the ground.

Once when I was working for a large multi-national company, I became involved in a plan to develop a set of new company values. I felt it was necessary to involve as many of the staff as possible; getting representatives to work in a significant number of geographic teams; facilitating cross-team communication and interaction; allowing them to produce a final list of four or five for the board of directors to rubber stamp. But long before I had developed some options I was notified of the five actual values from the board. They had already decided on the values, before our work was done. And unfortunately, many of the staff became cynical and responded with 'Well, let's see how long they live by them.' And because the values were handed down from on high, they weren't taken to heart. Nor were they followed.

Avoid banal slogans. And don't order badges, coffee mugs, pens or coasters with any new messages emblazed upon them. Often these publicity vehicles get widely distributed, in the hope that the message on them will be promoted and discussed. It won't, so save your money. And avoid money as an incentive at all costs – the change should be 'the right thing to do'. If it is, then the people will gladly accept it. The vast majority of people want to do the right thing.

So, to summarize. Managing effective change requires the appropriate level of everyday leadership, and leadership isn't meaningful unless it creates significant change. Good luck.

Question. What would you like to change? List the problems and challenges that you will face.

Name the change you would like to see
Problems and challenges

The Everyday Leader can describe the changes in detail and leads discussions to mitigate the unintentional pit-falls and knock-on effects.
The Everyday Leader doesn't assume that others have genuinely understood what is being asked of them, and constantly checks for their feelings and any misunderstandings.

15

Leading vision

This chapter asks you, the everyday leader, to think about your own ambitions and your own future; to think about how you might join forces with your friends in your local community to envision the improvements you would all like to see; and for those who work in organizations, to imagine a secure and successful future.

Establishing your personal vision

Davina McCall hosts a series on UK television called 'This Time Next Year', which features ordinary people on a mission to transform their lives or those closest to them, in a twelve-month window. In the first episode, Davina meets a woman with a pledge to lose ten stone (or 140 pounds).

The programme features ordinary members of the public who have decided to radically change something in their lives and come out publicly to announce it. In short they have decided upon a personal goal and they are determined to achieve it in the course of a year. For some it is less about themselves and more about others, e.g. Mum and

Dad are on a mission to provide their child, who was born profoundly deaf, with the ability to hear. Although twelve months is a short timeframe for many goals in life, it is a very worthwhile exercise to set a goal, communicate it to a wide audience, and then work out a plan of how to succeed. My question in this chapter is, 'Then what?' You have lost ten stone, your child can hear; what will you do next? This chapter is about fitting some of these types of short-term goals, into a longer-term flexible plan that houses *all* of your hopes and dreams. In other words, it asks people to articulate a 'vision' of the world they wish to create for themselves and others, and then to dispense with all objectives that do not fall under this over-arching goal.

As parents, we often ask our children, and those of relatives and close friends, 'what do you want to be when you grow up?' Answers typically involve fun and meaningful occupations such as becoming an astronaut, an artist, a musician, a police officer, a train driver, working with animals, etc. I've never known any child say, 'I'd like to work in an office.' Kids start out wanting excitement and fulfilment in their lives but some end up saddled with meaningless deadlines and dead-end jobs.

Is it that we change once we become adults? I have not changed (hence my learning to drive a large truck) and I don't think most us change that much either. Motorcycle speedway is next up on my list (though please don't tell my partner just yet!).

Perhaps you have a vision for your personal future and are working towards it. If you have, that's great, please enter it here:

....

....

....

However, if you do not know where you are going, then, as my mate, Des Lee says, 'any road will take you there'. Here are some of the questions that you may wish to consider and discuss with those closest to you.

1. Are you prepared to dream, and imagine a 'one day I will' scenario?
2. Are you happy? If yes, why? If no, why?
3. Are you content with your life and fulfilled by your experiences?
4. Can you differentiate between your 'needs' and 'wants' and prioritize the 'needs'?
5. What are your main interests or passions?
6. What are the values that you try to live by?
7. How do you continue to learn, and exercise your brain?
8. How do you look after your body?
9. How do you look after your spirit?
10. How do you have fun?
11. How do you relax?
12. Are you prepared to consider developing visions for the short, medium and longer term?
13. Are you prepared to let your imagination and desires run free and set outrageous visions?
14. Are you prepared, for the moment, to forget all of the things that may restrict or prevent you from realizing your ambitions?

Geoff Whitington (see Chapter 3) had a vision of death. Now he has a vision of helping diabetics to become free of the condition. Some of the above questions apply to you alone, whereas answers to others may involve a wider audience, partners and perhaps children. You will have read about parents selling up, buying a yacht, and then taking their children on a voyage around the world, taking several years to complete the circumnavigation. You will have read about other parents taking the whole family to make a long-term commitment to help villagers in the developing world. All they wanted was be free from what they perceived as the daily grind, and the shackles of conformity. They developed and owned these visions over several years before realizing their dream. Other visions could involve more or less change, but the point is to begin articulating one sooner rather than later. Below are some tools to get you started.

Some visioning exercises

Your short-term plans

Let's start with the short term: what do you want to achieve? For yourself, the usual suspects are eating less junk food, giving up smoking, drinking less, etc. It's natural to think about those things that you may want to *stop*, but also think about those that you may want to *start* doing. And what about the family unit or work team? What would you like to achieve, collectively, in the short term? Think of some options for stopping and starting that could begin tomorrow. Write them down here:

. . . .

. . . .

. . . .

. . . .

. . . .

. . . .

Make a list of your passions

Now have a think about passions and interests. What options can you list for yourself, your partner, your colleagues, or your children? Do you have an interest in vintage motorcars, or would you like to play the piano or a guitar?

. . . .

. . . .

. . . .

. . . .

. . . .

. . . .

If you were invited on to Davina McCall's show 'This Time Next Year', what would you choose from the list of things above? When you decide, it is important to declare the single item or list of things publicly, and ask for support to achieve them. The rewards from doing so will emerge immediately, as having decided on a personal vision or mission statement, you will feel your life becoming more focused and directed. Decisions, both minor and major, will be easier as you will measure their impact, both positive and negative, against your vision.

Your medium and long-term plans

But keep all of the options open for the moment until you decide upon a medium-term, and a longer-term vision. Then you may be able to identify a common thread, even a 'golden thread' that links all of the timescales together.

So, in the medium-term, say three-to-five years, what are your options?

....

....

....

....

....

....

And in the longer term, say ten-to-fifteen years, what are your dreams?

....

....

....

....

....

....

Some lessons from the personal visioning exercise

I knew someone whose whole life was devoted to one outcome: to prove his father wrong when he had said, 'You'll never be as good as your brother.' He became a workaholic and someone intent on career success.

I knew someone who spent a lifetime trying to trace and contact their sister who had been given up for adoption as a baby.

I knew someone who has adversely affected their appearance by undergoing cosmetic surgery in an attempt to be the most beautiful person they could be.

I watched the news one day to see two seniors; the man aged 91 at the time, and his wife then aged 89, emigrating to New Zealand. When asked why by the television reporter, they replied, 'to start a new life'. Good on them!

I travelled with someone today whose longer-term vision was to be mortgage-free in ten years.

Probably you know people whose life is dictated by a single objective; they may dream of buying a home abroad; or are preparing to enter an endurance road race through Asia. Where would we be without hopes and dreams? Some people re-visit their visions every year or two, because visions set as a teenager, need to change with adulthood, and then those need to adapt to the addition of more responsibilities at home and at work, and then change again as you start to reflect on your lifestyle in retirement.

You may have a secret vision or personal ambition. But without telling those around you about your plan, and your commitment to it, you drastically reduce your chances of success. Why? Because your friends and colleagues will remind you of it regularly, and urge you to take the next step in your plan. They will encourage and motivate you, even when your inner determination is flagging. Tell them.

Establishing a shared vision

A few miles out of Cambridge, England, lies the small village of Thriplow. It has a pub called The Green Man and a small shop. In 2012, 'The Green Man' was bought by a consortium of local supporters who formed a limited liability company (LLC) and issued shares to 90 people, raising £337,000. Triggered initially by a handful of local people discussing the possibility and viability of the village itself owning the pub, concerted local action has secured a sustainable future for a valued community asset and brought the villagers closer, with many making new friends in the process. This was everyday leadership in action in a small English village.

In Wales, in another village of a similar size, the residents of Michaelston y Fedw, became fed up with miserable internet connectivity. They couldn't bank online or download films, and despite numerous requests for improvements over many years, nothing was done by town council or the big telephone companies. So they decided to do it for themselves. And the only way was to dig miles of trenches in which to lay the cables. And dig it they did! Hundreds of villagers took part, volunteering to put in thousands of hours of hard labour to win a 1,000mps broadband connection.

Ben Longman, landlord of the Cefn Mably Arms, said: 'We were in the pub and we were all moaning about how bad the wifi was.' They came to realize that, unlike in the movies, the cavalry never arrives. So, if they were to join the twenty-first century, they had to do it themselves. Everyday leadership in action in a small Welsh village. As in Thriplow, new friendships were forged during these communal endeavours, bringing the whole community closer together.

And this type of shared visioning and community action is alive and well all over the world. Volunteers bring fresh water and sanitation to deprived areas in remote parts of the world, and nearer to home, youth clubs are started by community activists who want the best for their local youngsters. Community action can be undertaken by groups of individuals coming together for the first time as well as by well-established groups working on common causes.

Pastor Mimi Asher has made, and continues to make, a substantial contribution to her south London, Brixton community estate, by engaging with the gangs that fight in the streets around her. She tries to stop the retaliatory stabbings and cares for those wounded. Three teenagers ended up living with her, and gradually through dialogue, she learned a lot about their world. Slowly, she persuaded them to come into her world, introducing them to the evangelical church she founded, the Word of Grace Ministries.

In Chapter 3, I urged you to help your teenage children, lost in the social media world, by joining with them in order to understand their story. Only then, when they believe that you understand the pleasures they enjoy in their world, can you attempt to persuade them to re-join you in yours. It was the same for Pastor Mimi, first she had to understand, and only then could she attempt to be understood.

Take a look outside your home, and what do you see? What improvements could be made; what do your neighbours complain about? Are there transport issues, or social issues that you, as the everyday leader, could start to lead a community response? I'd be very surprised if there weren't.

Establishing a vision at work for supervisors, team members and managers

You are leading your team, or perhaps several teams, so what is your vision for the whole group? You could tell me about your set of objectives for the financial year, your key performance indicators (KPIs), and tell me that your vision is to achieve all of them. For projects that means finishing on time, to specification, and on budget. Great. That's fine, no problem. Not every vision has to be grandiose and transformational.

But there are two more areas I'd like you to think about. The first one centres around people. What sort of team spirit, 'esprit de corps', would make your team the best performing team? The team that everyone else wants to join? In short, do you have a vision for the spirit of the team against which you measure all of the decisions you have to make?

The second area is about meaning and purpose. The global pharmaceutical company, Astra Zeneca, is building a new head office in Cambridge, England, encouraging closer working relationships and faster progress by bringing together staff from a number of different geographic locations. I imagine that the vision of the team (the architects, planners, interior designers etc.) behind this building project could be, perhaps, 'To build a world-class structure that creates the environment in which our team can celebrate the successful design of better medicines.' Doing good, achieving something that is worthwhile, meaningful and valuable.

I have learned that the drivers of the trucks in which the Formula 1 Ferrari racing cars are transported between venues are paid a below-average wage. Obviously there are additional benefits to the job that compensate, including the kudos of being trusted with a multi-million dollar truck on the narrow winding roads of Europe and beyond. But if I were the team leader of an F1 team I would make those truck drivers the most highly paid in the world. The number of drivers is small and the extra cost is negligible when compared to their improved status and the newly bestowed bragging rights. Famous for being above-average and not below-average is a goal to aspire to as an employer. Decide the reputation you want.

Establishing a work vision for senior executives and your organization

When I had a group of senior civil servants in a room, I asked them to introduce themselves and to describe, in turn, what they did for 'me' (i.e. a local resident paying taxes, who was married with adult children and grandchildren). All failed. Instead, they described what they did in general non-personal terms and never once articulated how their work contributed to the well-being of the citizens they ultimately served.

Vehicle rental company Avis has a vision statement that states, 'We will lead our industry by defining service excellence and building unmatched customer loyalty.' The focus on customer satisfaction is great, but apart from mentioning 'loyalty', it lacks emotional impact. My alternative options would be, 'We want to be the best-loved vehicle rental company in the world.' Or 'We want to be the most-loved rental company in the world. Or 'We want to be the best-loved company in the world.'

As Amazon grew, they changed visions from wanting to be 'the world's largest book seller', to 'the world largest retailer'. But does being the 'largest' at anything necessarily equate to being the 'best'? That is not so clear.

Look closely at the vision for your organization. Does it speak to the staff, to the customers and to the industry? Does it state what success looks like or feels? How ambitious is the vision? To be the best in 'your world' could mean within a town, region or country. It could be within your regional or global industry. Or it could be a level of customer satisfaction for all industries. Whatever it is, or whatever you make it, it is rather important because it becomes the yardstick against which you measure all of the decisions that are made every day within your organization. It determines your strategy.

Solving problems for your users and satisfying your customers has to be the main target for all commercial organizations. Without it the business won't be able to grow market share, and without that, the business won't be able to secure the best margins. Not-for-profit organizations also need to address delivery and stakeholder engagement.

Scale is often important when sending messages. Using the word 'large' – like Amazon – often implies impersonal, while making a point of being 'small' can sometimes imply being more expensive. What is your business or organization famous for? You have a reputation for what? If you conducted a poll among your staff, what percentage would be able to quote your vision for the future? How many of Avis' 30,000 employees would be able to recall theirs? The answer is probably not that many.

The problem often with corporate visioning is a lack of emotional connectivity. Below are some examples of organizational visions, on a broad scale, that work by connecting on an individual level.

Examples of organizational visions that make a connection

Soldiers of the 1st Battalion, the Royal Irish Regiment in Iraq in 2003, could repeat their Commanding Officer's words on the eve of the allied invasion for many years after. Many could do it verbatim. Colonel Tim Collins started with the poignant words: 'We go to liberate, not to conquer.' I will not repeat it all here save to say that it was the most brilliant expression of intent.[1] Tim had a vision, which was so carefully and elegantly crafted that it still leaves tears in the eyes and a lump in the throat.

In World War 2, the allied air forces in South East Asia were under the command of a senior Royal Air Force Officer, Richard Peirse, and his American number two, Major-General George Stratemeyer. George issued the following vision of how the British and American air forces would integrate and work together: 'We must merge into one unified force, in thought and in deed, neither English, nor American, with the faults of neither and the virtues of both . . .' So well said.

Barclays Bank, in the wake of the Global Financial Crisis, established a reformulated common purpose that is certainly more emotive than most banks: 'Creating opportunities to rise.' 'We are a company of opportunity makers working together to help people rise – customers, clients, colleagues and society.'

Examples of organizational visions that don't work so well

I like the use of the word 'best', but not on its own – best what? Best value, best quality, best . . .? For example, the Kraft Heinz vision is 'to be the best food company, growing a better world'. But I'm less enthusiastic about 'growing a better world'. I don't understand what that means. Do you?

Coca Cola has really gone to town with their recent vision statement. They say:

> *Coca Cola's vision 'serves as the framework for our Roadmap and guides every aspect of our business by describing what we need to accomplish in order to continue achieving sustainable, quality growth.*
>
> > *People: Be a great place to work where people are inspired to be the best they can be.*
> >
> > *Portfolio: Bring to the world a portfolio of quality beverage brands that anticipate and satisfy people's desires and needs.*
> >
> > *Partners: Nurture a winning network of customers and suppliers, together we create mutual, enduring value.*
> >
> > *Planet: Be a responsible citizen that makes a difference by helping build and support sustainable communities.*
> >
> > *Profit: Maximize long-term return to shareowners while being mindful of our overall responsibilities.*
> >
> > *Productivity: Be a highly effective, lean and fast-moving organization.'*

I wonder why they felt the need to have all bullets start with the letter 'P'? Is this list inspiring to consumers? Is it motivating for employees?

Contrast the Coca Cola statement with the Rolls-Royce vision: 'Rolls-Royce pioneers cutting edge technologies that deliver the cleanest, safest and most competitive solutions to meet our planet's vital power needs.' It works not only because of its brevity and focus, as compared to Coke, but because it talks about solving problems and connects with things people care about. And it uses 'clean*est*, saf*est* and *most* competitive' to state its determination to be the best.

The essential qualities of a great vision statement

So let's have a look at what I believe are the essential qualities and characteristics of a well-formed vision statement:

- Memorable and repeatable.
- Success looks like this . . .
- Paints a vivid mental picture.
- Inspirational to all those close and worthy to those more distant.
- Short.
- Concise.
- Differentiated.
- Avoids management-speak and jargon.
- Contains emotions, feelings, passion.
- Timeline – about five years or so.
- Made personal.

If those are the desirable qualities, let me attempt to construct a vision for a local café that has just opened up in your neighbourhood:

> We are striving to make your visit with us memorable for the warmth of our welcome, the great and unique taste of our products, and the efficiency of our service, that when you're next thirsty or hungry you think of us first.

I've made it personal, 'you' and 'yours'. I've got feelings and emotions, 'warmth', 'taste', 'thirsty' and 'hungry'. I have defined the three most important dimensions on which the staff can focus upon: i) the welcome; ii) the great and unique taste/flavours; and iii) the efficient service. Customers can measure their satisfaction with their coffee, breakfast or lunchtime snack using the same criteria.

If you're not happy with my statement, try to improve my effort here:

....

....

....

....

....

Imagine that you have taken over as the owner of a local florist, hairdresser or baker. You meet with your staff to create your own vision. What will it be?

....

....

....

....

....

And then why not use this exercise as an introduction to your colleagues before examining the vision for your own organization, team and family. Good luck.

Question. Name one of your dreams and asks others to name one of their dreams.

One of your dreams
Your partner's?
One of your friend's?
One of your work colleague's?

The Everyday Leader helps others to fulfil their hopes and dreams for the future.
The Everyday Leader doesn't miss opportunities to ask others where they see themselves in a year or two or more so that their 'story' is better understood.

The 'opportunity' chapter

Thank you for reaching this point. We didn't want to call it a conclusion, because it's not the end of something but rather a beginning. You have read what my colleagues and I have put together and you may have already changed some of your approaches and some of your thinking. Opportunities to exercise and experiment with our recommendations may have already presented themselves to you, but if not they soon will. We have offered you many different models of how you might approach tricky everyday leadership situations. They have been forged by the lessons learned by our own trials and errors, combined failures and disappointments over the years. We, and others like us, have made the mistakes so that you don't have to.

You should now be a lot more self-conscious – in a good way – about your role as an everyday leader. After reading this book, you are now setting a better example to your friends and colleagues. But the lessons we have offered don't need to be kept private; share them with family, friends and work colleagues. At the end of every chapter we have asked you some questions; these may not have a quick or easy answer, but will hopefully trigger a discussion or conversation from which you will be handsomely rewarded, often with much more information and knowledge than you had dared to know or find out.

If Rafael, Kevin and I know one thing, it's that we're not always right. But nor are we always wrong. We have designed a leadership toolkit for everyday leaders like you, but we understand that you will need to twist and shape the detail so that it fits your circumstances more precisely than we could ever imagine.

We recommend that you read and re-read Chapters 1 and 15 regularly. Chapter 1 so that you can ask those closest to you for a 'progress report' on the changes that you have decided to make; recording and dating the comments that you receive can provide some intrinsic reward for the effort you are making. And if you maintain the record over the long term, and casually glance at it occasionally, you will be able to mentally re-visit those moments when you made a difference. Chapter 15 is worth re-reading so that you can regularly bring the 'big picture' into your everyday activities and make more small steps towards the achievement of your dreams.

We wish you well on your continuing leadership journey.

NOTES

Chapter 1

1 www.cricket.com.au/news/cricket-australia-cultural-review-published-recommendations-ethics-players-south-africa-smith-warner/ 2018-10-29

2 The neocortex is involved in higher functions such as sensory perception, generation of motor commands, spatial reasoning, conscious thought, and in humans, language. The cerebral neocortex is the entire outer top part of the brain (the part that looks wrinkled when we view a brain in images or in models). The prefrontal cortex is that part of the neocortex at the very front of the brain. It is involved in 'executive functions' such as planning, goals, and actions.

Read the full *Guardian* story 'Richard Thaler is a controversial Nobel prize winner – but a deserving one' link at: https://www.theguardian.com/world/2017/oct/11/richard-thaler-nobel-prize-winner-behavioural-economics.

Several books explain the science behind our inner voice battle and what we can do about it, some of the best are:

Thaler, R. and Sunstein, C. (2008). *Nudge: Improving Decisions about Health, Wealth, and Happiness.* Yale University Press.

Ariely, D. (2008). *Predictably Irrational: The Hidden Forces That Shape Our Decisions.* New York: HarperCollins.

Kahneman, D. (2011). *Thinking, Fast and Slow.* New York: Farrar, Straus and Giroux.

3 Take a look at: www.thelondoneconomic.com/news/watch-tessa-jowell-receives-standing-ovation-house-lords-moving-speech/26/01/ to witness Lord Bassam's brief struggle with his inner voices. When resolved Lord Bessam became a 'first mover'. Have you let others take the lead when you yourself felt restricted? And if so, why was that? And while you're logged on, take a look at https://www.youtube.com/watch?v=GA8z7f7a2Pk to see the famous 'dancing man' 'first mover'. The three-minute video has enjoyed over 15 million views, and deservedly so.

4 https://fondation.vinci-autoroutes.com/fr/article/parentalite-au-volant-quand-les-enfants-reproduisent-les-comportements-de-leurs-parents-sur

5 www.theiet.org/media/press-releases/press-releases-2018/07-june-2018-parents-put-children-off-studying-stem/

Chapter 2

1 www.rotherham.gov.uk/downloads/file/1407/independent_inquiry_cse_in_rotherham and www.gov.uk/government/publications/report-of-inspection-of-rotherham-metropolitan-borough-council

2 I recommend people read the entire story of Ms Bloomfield and the near collapse of her food empire, all because of her inability to listen and observe what was going on in her restaurant. The full story, aptly titled 'Breaking the Silence on Abuse' can be found in the *New York Times* International Edition. See: Moskin, Julia and Kim Severson (2018) 'Breaking the Silence on Abuse', *The New York Times (International Edition)*. 2—21 October, pp. 7–8.

3 A wonderful and inspiring obituary of Ian Kiernan's accomplishments appeared in the *New York Times* International Edition in late October 2018. The journalist quotes Terrie-Ann Johnson, the managing director of Clean Up Australia, the organization Mr Kiernan started with a group of friends in 1990. According to Ms Johnson Ian was imbued with a non-nonsense down-to-earth attitude. Quoting Ms Johnson directly, Ian apparently 'hated people who would pontificate and rattle on about things; he just wanted to get it done.' Pretty much the definition of the everyday leader we've been talking about. See: Albeck-Ripka, Livia. (2018). 'Record Setting Australian Sailor Who Battled Pollution', *The New York Times* (International Edition), 20–21 October, p. 2.

4 Much has been written about Margaret Mead, who was a pioneer in the field of Anthropology in the early 1920s and 1930s. Some of her legacy is controversial given that she studied what were then called 'primitive societies' from a decidedly Western lens. But there is no doubt that she was a first-rate 'observer' of human behaviour and a real role model for women scholars to this day. For a thorough account of her life and work I would recommend the following book: Lutkehaus, Nancy C. (2008) *Margaret Mead: The Making of an American Icon*. Princeton: Princeton University Press.

Chapter 3

1 Dan Pink, the popular writer and Ted Talk speaker has done a lot to popularise the power of purpose in our daily lives and inside of organizations. His book, *Drive: The Surprising Truth About What Motivates Us*, is an accessible window into the world of academic research surrounding human motivation, but it is actual researchers like Adam Grant that have done the hard work of proving that 'purpose' works. See: Grant, A. M. (2008) The significance of task significance: Job performance effects, relational mechanisms, and boundary conditions. *Journal of Applied Psychology*, *93*(1), 108.

2 Papps, K. L., Bryson, A. and Gomez, R. (2011). Heterogeneous worker ability and team-based production: Evidence from major league baseball, 1920–2009, *Labour Economics*, 18(3), 310–319.

Jackson, P. (2004). 'The Soul of Teamwork.' *Enlighten Next Magazine*, May–July 2004.

www.enlightennext.org/magazine/j25/teamwork.asp, accessed on March 10, 2010.

Chapter 4

1 The violent riot held in central London in March 1990 opposing the Poll Tax made global headlines, and did much to contribute to the downfall of Margaret Thatcher, who resigned as Prime Minister on 28 November of the same year. The national opposition to the poll tax was especially vehement in northern England and Scotland, but the anger over the tax cut across most political and income lines. An opinion poll at the time found 78 per cent opposed it. For more see the excellent National Archives section of the BBC online which recounts the events surrounding the Poll Tax and how it brought down one of Britain's longest serving Prime Ministers. See: www.bbc.com/news/uk-38382416, accessed October 2018.

2 Frank updated his book in 2010, to account for the aftermath of the Great Recession. See: Frank, Robert H. (2010) *Luxury Fever Weighing the Cost of Excess*. New Jersey: Princeton University Press.

3 www.siobhainmcdonagh.org.uk/campaigns/sainsburys-work-well-for-less.aspx

4 www.cipd.co.uk/knowledge/fundamentals/relations/engagement/employee-outlook-reports

5 www.barnett-waddingham.co.uk/comment-insight/research/2018/11/12/why-bwell-wellbeing-workplace/

6 This reference to de Bono and his 'red hat' is to the system designed by Edward de Bono, which describes a tool for group discussion and individual thinking involving six coloured hats. Six distinct 'mental' directions are identified and assigned a colour. The six directions are:

- **Managing** (Blue) – what is the subject? What are we thinking about? What is the goal? Look at the big picture.
- **Information** (White) – considering purely what information is available, what are the facts?
- **Emotions** (Red) – intuitive or instinctive gut reactions or statements of emotional feeling (but not any justification).
- **Discernment** (Black) – logic applied to identifying reasons to be cautious and conservative, lists what can go wrong with any new idea. Practical, realistic.
- **Optimistic response** (Yellow) – logic applied to identifying benefits, seeking harmony, lists what can go right with any new idea. Sees the brighter, sunny side of situations.
- **Creativity** (Green) – statements of provocation and investigation, seeing where a thought goes. Thinks creatively, outside the box.

Coloured hats are used as metaphors for each direction but in practice, training sessions can literally involve putting on a hat or wearing the colour of your assigned mental direction. de Bono, now in his 80s is still active as a writer, management professor and world-renowned consultant who in the 1970s helped coin the term 'lateral thinking' but his most famous work is still the 'Six Thinking Hats'. That idea, along with the associated idea of 'parallel thinking', provides a means for groups to plan processes in a detailed and cohesive way, and to work together more effectively. It's a tool I have used in my own training practice and it works every time, especially the more sceptical the audience trying it is!

See: de Bono, Edward (1985) *Six Thinking Hats: An Essential Approach to Business Management*. Little, Brown, & Company.

7 There is a wide variety of papers showing the benefits to firms of employee

involvement. One of us has recently published a paper looking across the Anglo-American world on the effect of employee involvement and found positive results. See: Wilkinson, Adrian, Michael Barry, Rafael Gomez and Bruce E Kaufman. (2018a) 'Taking the pulse at work: An employment relations scorecard for Australia', *Journal of Industrial Relations*. Vol. 60, Issue 2, pp. 145–175. And recently the UK government has advocated for more involvement from employees at work, so this is not just an academic exercise anymore. See: O'Connor, S. (2017) 'Taylor Report to Call for More 'Voice' for UK Workers'. *Financial Times*, 7 July 2017. Downloaded at: www.ft.come/content/422b3c9a-6248-11e7-91a7-502f7ee26895

8 www.buddhanet.net/e-learning/qanda02.htm

Chapter 5

1 Interesting to note that this may be Gallic cultural trait that has become ingrained since the time of the Enlightenment. A popular parenting book by Pamela Druckerman called Bringing Up Bébé describes many of the same approaches outlined by Rousseau in Emile. Druckerman is an American mom living in Paris bringing up her children and observing the contrast in American versus French approaches. One of the keys to French parenting (which she admires greatly) is what Druckerman refers to as keeping children inside the 'cadre' – or literally inside the 'box' in English. The idea is that kids are seemingly given a lot more scope for free 'reign' in France but never in an environment that has not been prescribed by the parent. In Druckerman's words 'Cadre means that kids have a lot of freedom, but within very firm limits – that's the frame [cadre] – and that the parents strictly enforce those limits. But within those limits, the kids should be free.' Sounds like Rousseau's still alive and well. There is no copyright protection for eighteenth-century manuscripts. I suggest you dip into Rousseau's Emile and find other interesting passages. See: www.philosophy-index.com/rousseau/emile/book-ii.php

2 https://assets.publishing.service.gov.uk/media/5422f0a5ed915d13710002fb/3-2003_HL-7451.pdf
www.nelsonmandela.org/content/page/biography
www.aljazeera.com/news/africa/2011/03/201131218852687848.html
www.constitution.org/mac/prince.pdf
http://ricardosemler.com/
http://alzheimersocietyblog.ca/making-difference-with-techology/

Chapter 6

1 www.youtube.com/watch?v=KDNPczXV14Y

2 See: Vozza, Stephanie. (2014) 'Why Amazon And Coca-Cola Have The Best Corporate Reputations?' *Fast Company*. 5 December 2014. Accessed: www.fastcompany.com/3030357/why-amazon-and-coca-cola-have-the-best-corporate-reputations

Chapter 7

1 The International Association of Athletics Federations (IAAF) Diamond League is an annual series of elite track and field athletic competitions. The series began with the 2010 IAAF Diamond League, which replaced the IAAF Golden League, which had been held annually since 1998. The Diamond League uses professional pacesetters in long-distance races ostensibly to improve runner performance. A pacesetter is typically someone who is in the lead during part of a race or competition and therefore decides the speed or standard of the race or competition for that time.

2 For more on Duncker and applications to the word of work, Dan Pink in his popular TED Talk spells out the problems with motivation that arise when we face Duncker 'Candle-type Problems'. I recommend you view the entire talk: www.ted.com/talks/dan_pink_on_motivation. For the original Duncker paper, see: Duncker, K. (1945) 'On problem solving', *Psychological Monographs*, 58: 5, p. 275.

3 William Goldman is now 87 years old but still active in Hollywood. He has won two Academy Awards for his screenplays, first for the western *Butch Cassidy and the Sundance Kid* (1969) and again for *All the President's Men* (1976), about journalists Carl Bernstein and Bob Woodward, who broke the Watergate scandal of President Richard Nixon for the *Washington Post*. His other notable works include his thriller novel *Marathon Man* and children's fantasy novel *The Princess Bride*, both of which Goldman adapted for film. His life-lessons were encapsulated in his book on Hollywood. See: Goldman, William (2001). *Which Lie Did I Tell?: More Adventures in the Screen Trade*. New York: Vintage.

4 Moore's Law is the observation made by Intel co-founder Gordon Moore that the number of transistors on a chip doubles every year while the costs

are halved. In 1965, Gordon Moore noticed that the number of transistors per square inch on integrated circuits had doubled every year since their invention. Today it has been popularized to describe how overall processing power for computers tends to double every two years.

5 For those wanting to learn more about how we have insights, and where inspiration comes from, I recommend you read 'The neuroscience of Bob Dylan's genius', by Jonah Lehrer published in *the Guardian* on Friday 6 April 2012: www.theguardian.com/music/2012/apr/06/neuroscience-bob-dylan-genius-creativity . Or read the full book, *Imagine: How Creativity Works*, by Jonah Lehrer, published by Canongate Books.

6 www.dartmouth.edu/press-releases/digital-media-change-050816.html

Chapter 8

1 Though popularized in the mid-1990s, emotional intelligence (EI) is a concept that was known to psychologists for some time prior to the publication of Goleman's best-selling book, appearing in 1983 as two of Howard Gardner's multiple intelligences under the guise of inter and intrapersonal skill and in a 1990 paper by social psychologists Peter Salovey and John Mayer titled simply 'Emotional Intelligence'. These works also were predated by a 1964 paper by Michael Beldoch in which the term 'emotional intelligence' was first used and defined. But interestingly, and illustrative of our concept of leading relationships, it wasn't until a journalist with an ability to communicate and relate to readers that the idea of EI took off. For more on EI see:

Beldoch, M. (1964) 'Sensitivity to expression of emotional meaning in three modes of communication', in J. R. Davitz et al., The Communication of Emotional Meaning, McGraw-Hill, pp. 31–42.

Salovey, P. and Mayer, J. D. (1990) 'Emotional Intelligence', *Imagination, Cognition and Personality*, 9(3), 185–211. https://doi.org/10.2190/DUGG-P24E-52WK-6CDG

Gardner, H. (1983) *Frames of Mind*. New York: Basic Books.

Goleman, D. (1995) *Emotional Intelligence*. New York: Bantam Books.

2 Research on social ties has really exploded since the advent of social networking. But the essence of ideas are still to be found in the original work by ground-breaking sociologists such as Mark Gronovetter and Ronald Burt.

See: Granovetter, M.S. (1983) 'The strength of weak ties: a network theory revisited', in R. Collins (Ed.), *Sociological Theory*. Jossey-Bass: San Francisco, CA. pp. 201–233.

3 https://waitrose.pressarea.com/pressrelease/details/78/NEWS_13/6485

Chapter 9

1 Robert Cialdini and his colleagues in a famous experiment showed that to activate social norms, people need to be told or shown the path forward, and crucially they have to be shown that they are also not alone. The experiment in question was aimed at reducing litter in public spaces. In one experiment the scale of the problem was shown (a picture of a dirty park and an overflowing rubbish bin) and then a message imploring readers to 'do something about it'. Next was a scene of thousands of volunteers cleaning parks across the city, with the message 'isn't it time you joined the call?' The second message proved to be the much more powerful motivator of action and led to a cleaner city park system.

See: Cialdini, R.B. (2003) 'Crafting normative messages to protect the environment', *Current Directions in Psychological Science*, 12(4), pp. 105–109.

2 In one of their classic studies James H. Fowler, and Nicholas A. Christakis measured the 'epidemic spread' of happiness. Specifically the authors set out to evaluate whether happiness can spread from person to person and whether niches of happiness form within social networks. The results of their study showed that clusters of happy and unhappy people are visible in the network, and the relationship between people's happiness extends up to three degrees of separation (for example, to the friends of one's friends' friends). People who are surrounded by many happy people and those who are central in the network are more likely to become happy in the future. Further analysis suggests that clusters of happiness result from the spread of happiness and not just a tendency for people to associate with similar individuals. A friend who lives within a mile (about 1.6 km) and who becomes happy increases the probability that a person is happy by 25 per cent. Similar effects are seen in co-resident spouses, siblings who live within a mile and next door neighbours. The punch line is that people's happiness depends on the happiness of others with whom they are connected. This provides further justification for seeing happiness, like health, as an 'epidemic' phenomenon.

See: Christakis, N.A. and Fowler, J.H. (2009). *Connected: The surprising power of our social networks and how they shape our lives.* New York: Little, Brown.

Chapter 10

1 A model that has emerged in the United States, which integrates health authorities with educational agencies has emphasized exactly this point: alignment and integration need to be thought of in tandem. The so-called Whole School, Whole Community, Whole Child (WSCC) model developed by a national educational organization (ASCD) and the US Centers for Disease Control (CDC), is a framework and a call for the health and education sectors to work toward greater alignment and coordination of policy, process, and practice. The WSCC model, released in 2014, was developed to ensure that school-community and education-health sector alignments are front and centre. Despite the strong connections, the health and education sectors have, for the most part, grown, developed, and established their influence independent of each other. Yet, they are often serving the same child, in the same location, and often attending separately to the same issues. The alignment, integration, and collaboration across health and education sectors therefore holds the potential for greater efficiency, reduced resource consumption, and improved outcomes for both sectors.

For a review of this approach see: Chiang, R. J., Meagher, W. and Slade, S. (2015). 'How the whole school, whole community, whole child model works: creating greater alignment, integration, and collaboration between health and education', *Journal of School Health*, *85*(11), 775–784.

Chapter 11

1 In a recent article by Sarah Todd with the elaborate title 'An economic theory developed in 1817 can help you cut your to-do list in half' she summarizes the findings of a book by Tiffany Dufu, author of *Drop the Ball: Achieving More by Doing Less*, which teaches readers about the theory of comparative advantage and how to deploy it at work and in personal settings. For example, Dofu writes in *Drop the Ball*, that 'as a seasoned nonprofit fund-raiser, I [thought I was] better than my staff at drafting annual fund letters,

but I brought the most value in face-to-face meetings pitching major donors. No one else on my team could do that.' So it made sense for her to let go of letter-writing – even if she was really good at it – and concentrate on forging connections with philanthropists. Dufu then realized, what I have argued above, that you could apply the theory to domestic settings as well. At the time, Dofu was frequently overwhelmed by her domestic responsibilities at work and as a spouse and the mother of a young child. So she scrutinized her to-do list, asking herself which were the tasks that only she could do in order to realize her major goal as a parent: to raise a conscious global citizen.

2 There is probably no voice in academia more knowledgeable and often cited on the topic of self-guidance and motivation than Professor Gary Latham from the University of Toronto. His seminal textbook *Work Motivation: History, Theory, Research, and Practice*, provides a unique behavioural science approach for motivating employees in organizational settings. Drawing, upon his experiences as a staff psychologist and consultant to organizations, he uses a 'mentor voice' to bring forth useful examples. He was one of the first management experts to see how the sport coaching tools of visualizing and self-talk could work with employee tasks and goals. See: Latham, G. P. (2012). *Work Motivation: History, Theory, Research, and Practice*. New York: Sage.

Chapter 12

1 A 2014 study, one of the first to examine helicopter-parenting on college-aged kids, found students who reported having over-controlling parents reported significantly higher levels of depression and less satisfaction with life. Furthermore, the negative effects of helicopter parenting on college students' well-being were largely explained by the perceived violation of students' basic psychological needs for autonomy and competence. For more, see: Schiffrin, H. H., Liss, M., Miles-McLean, H., Geary, K. A., Erchull, M. J. and Tashner, T. (2014) 'Helping or hovering? The effects of helicopter parenting on college students' well-being', *Journal of Child and Family Studies*, 23(3), 548–557.

2 van Ingen, D. J., Freiheit, S. R., Steinfeldt, J. A., Moore, L. L., Wimer, D. J., Knutt, A. D. and Roberts, A. (2015) 'Helicopter parenting: The effect of an overbearing caregiving style on peer attachment and self-efficacy', *Journal of College Counseling*, 18(1), 7–20.

3 Most research into 'snowflake' syndrome and entitlement treats it as a personality trait, not exploring the role played by environment in

conditioning people to feel overly entitled or sensitive. Recent research explores how environment can create a sense of over-entitlement in subjects. See: Lastner, M. and Taylor, E. (2015). The Snowflake State: An Investigation into Entitlement as a State Construct. In *Academy of Management Proceedings*, Vol. 2015, No. 1, p. 15108.

4 Check out her website: https://honestmum.com. Her book was chosen by the *Independent* as one of the 10 best business books written by women in 2018. The tag line for her book, reads somewhat fittingly: 'Vicki is one inspirational mumboss, who shares her secrets to juggling a thriving business with raising a family in this entertaining and empowering read!'

5 For the actual study upon which the HBR article (cited in note 1) was based see: Lee, A., Willis, S. and Tian, A. W. (2018) 'Empowering leadership: A meta-analytic examination of incremental contribution, mediation, and moderation', *Journal of Organizational Behavior*, 39(3), 306–325.

6 The 'Corner Office' feature in the *New York Times* is usually filled with interesting stories like that of Mr Ulukaya. See: Gelles, David (2018) 'Greek Yogurt Fulfilled an American Dream', *New York Times*, Sunday 26 August 2018, p. 3.

Chapter 13

1 For more on this emotionally wrought story, see: http://webarchive.nationalarchives.gov.uk/20150407084003/http://www.midstaffspublicinquiry.com/

2 In 1975, Professor Steven Kerr wrote a famous article in the *Academy of Management Journal* titled, 'On the folly of rewarding A, while hoping for B' that's become a management classic. Over the decades, this article has been widely admired for its relevance and insight. The article (there is the 1975 original and a 1995 update that is linked below) provides many excellent examples of situations where the reward structure subtly (or sometimes blatantly) undermines the ultimate goal being set. See the 1995 updated of the original article here: www.ou.edu/russell/UGcomp/Kerr.pdf

3 An iconoclastic thinker in economic and political theory, Albert O. Hirschman made a basic distinction between alternative ways of reacting to deterioration in customer service and, in general, to dissatisfaction with

organizations: 'exit', happens when a member quits the organization or for the customer to switch to a competing product, and 'voice', is for members or customers to agitate and exert influence for change 'from within'. The efficiency of the competitive mechanism, with its total reliance on exit, is questioned by Hirschman in a number of important situations. Because exit often undercuts voice, making an organization unable to counteract decline, loyalty is seen in the function of retarding exit and of permitting voice to play its proper role in fixing a problem and improving product/service quality.

Chapter 14

1 The work of Tversky and Khaneman is legendary in the field of what has become known as behavioural economics. Their original paper is amazing for its breadth and applicability even today. For more see: Tversky, Amos and Daniel Kahneman (1974) 'Judgment under uncertainty: Heuristics and biases', *Science*, Vol. 185, Issue 4157, pp. 1124–1131.

2 Text of the report on the railway upgrade failure can be found here: http://orr.gov.uk/rail/consumers/inquiry-into-may-2018-network-disruption

3 An excellent timeline of the crisis at TSB was provided by *the Guardian* here: www.theguardian.com/business/2018/jun/06/timeline-of-trouble-how-the-tsb-it-meltdown-unfolded

4 https://skyoceanrescue.com/

Chapter 15

1 The eve-of-battle speech made by Colonel Tim Collins to the 1st Battalion of the Royal Irish Regiment in Iraq in 2003 was published in 2008 for the first time. Here is the copy available on the *Telegraph* website: www.telegraph.co.uk/comment/3562917/Colonel-Tim-Collins-Iraq-war-speech-in-full.html

INDEX